# ITALIAN
## *Food Artisans*
### Traditions and Recipes

In celebration of
artisan traditions

*Pamela Sheldon Johns*

# ITALIAN
# *Food Artisans*

## Traditions and Recipes

### by Pamela Sheldon Johns

*Photographs by John Rizzo*

**CHRONICLE BOOKS**

SAN FRANCISCO

*This book is dedicated to the memory of my father, who shared many of the attributes I found in the artisans profiled here: a sense of quality, dedication to purpose, and attention to detail.*

*To my dear husband, Courtney, for his uncompromising support and love.*

*And to my daughter, Alaia Rose, with the hope that all of these wonderful foods will be available for her and her children.*

Text copyright © 2000 by Pamela Sheldon Johns.
All photographs copyright © 2000 by John Rizzo except for the following: pages 86–88, 90, 91, 93 by Colette Conforti; pages 60 (lower right), 120–22, 136, 162 by Pamela Sheldon Johns; page 139 by Richard Jung; pages 15–16, 17 (lower left), 152, 160 by Nicola Lorusso; pages 21, 99, 123, author photo by Ingo Markmann; page 153 by Pierpaolo Pagano.

Library of Congress Cataloging-in-Publication Data:
    Johns, Pamela Sheldon, 1953-
    Italian food artisans : traditions and recipes / by Pamela Sheldon Johns.
    168 p.    21 x 23 cm.
    Includes bibliographical references and index.
    ISBN 0-8118-2129-3 (hardcover)
    1. Cookery, Italian. 2. Food habits—Italy. I. Title.
    TX723.J64    2000
    394.1'0945—dc21        99–17659
                      CIP

Printed in Hong Kong.

Designed by Franke Design
Typeset in Hoefler Text and Florens with Zapf Dingbats

Distributed in Canada by Raincoast Books
8680 Cambie Street
Vancouver, British Columbia V6P 6M9

10 9 8 7 6 5 4 3 2 1

Chronicle Books
85 Second Street
San Francisco, California 94105

www.chroniclebooks.com

# ACKNOWLEDGMENTS

Thank you first to the artisans and their families for giving their time and opening their lives to me.

Friends, friends of friends, word-of-mouth; many sources have led me to rediscover some of the original tastes that I remember from my first visit to Italy.

I found many artisans through connections made with artisan-food importer Rolando Beramendi and our collaboration on culinary programs. I owe a large debt, also, to a wonderful Italian guide called *Il Buon Paese*. This geographic listing of top-quality food producers is published by Slow Food (see Resources, page 163), an association dedicated to fighting fast food.

Many individuals were instrumental in assisting me in the collection of information. I extend a heartfelt thanks to Lucy De Fazio, Kimberly Wicks Bartolozzi, Marina Donà dalle Rose, Leo Bertozzi, Mario Zannoni, Nancy Radke, Carol van Wonterghem, Alberto Falvo, Riccardo Bertocci, Angelo Palmieri, Nicolino Palmieri, Alessandra Peres, and Ed Valenzuela.

My colleagues who have trod this ground before me offered literary and friendly support: thank you, especially, to Burton Anderson, Nancy Harmon Jenkins, and Carol Field.

Alaia and I both thank our traveling companions Linda Hale and Gioia Bartoli-Cardi.

My appreciation to Leslie Jonath for taking an intense interest in this topic and seeing it to its finished form, along with Sharon Silva and Mikyla Bruder. Kisses to Anne Dickerson for putting us together, and to my literary agent, Jane Dystel, for her support.

At home, I couldn't have done it without the help of my recipe testers Gioia Bartoli-Cardi and Philippa Farrar, along with home testers Linda Hale, Mari Kay Bartoli, Judy Dawson, Paula Ferguson, and Diane Townsend. Thank you to my "readers," Carla Mengel, Janice Ross, Robert Zeman, Keri Jo Moore, Jennifer Barry, and, of course, Courtney.

And, finally, to my mother, thank you for your patience and support.

# CONTENTS

# INTRODUCTION

I am half Italian, although you might never know it. I didn't know it myself until I was thirty. Adopted at birth, I grew up in suburban Southern California, experiencing a wonderful childhood with summers on Catalina Island and winter weekends and holidays in the desert on land that my father homesteaded.

My midwestern mother was a very good cook, and my father had a marvelous garden. I learned to appreciate seasonal produce as I ran from the garden, clutching three ears of corn, to the pot of boiling water, anxious for the taste of kernels full of natural sweetness. It was a sensibility that prepared me to love Italy.

My first visit to Italy was in 1983, a grand camping tour with two girlfriends. In my journal I wrote, "This feels like a place I've always known. It may be just that the weather, the land, the food, and even the people are all perfectly to my taste." I became a student of everything Italian, but particularly the food. I was intrigued by the essence of taste in even the simplest of ingredients, and knew that I would want to recreate the same flavors once I returned home. Back in Southern California, my dream quickly faded. The proper ingredients were scarce, something was missing. So, I returned to Italy. This time I brought an empty suitcase, not for leather jackets and shoes, but for olive oil, cheese, dried porcini, truffle oil, and balsamic vinegar. It's a funny habit that I still engage in, even though many of these ingredients are now available in the United States.

In the past fifteen years, I have sensed a shift in flavors in Italy. Perhaps it was the romance of the virgin taste, my rapture at being there for the first time, but I could swear some things tasted better in 1983. I hear others with deeper experience than mine say the same thing.

Standards for the way foods are produced and marketed are changing rapidly everywhere, and it would be presumptuous for me, an outsider, to insist that the Italians must work harder to protect their traditions. Indeed, they are already trying to do just that at many levels, and the result is that a tiny niche of local artisans are making their products in limited quantities. These remarkable producers—passionate and dedicated to a single goal—exist in delightful abundance in the smaller villages, but theirs is a number that is diminishing.

Will the traditions be carried on? It is difficult to say. It depends in large part on one's definition of "a better life." Is it one rich in tradition or one in which all creature comforts and material desires are met?

Life is changing in Italy, just as it is all over the world. It's hard to ignore technology, especially when it saves us time and money. The European Union is working to standardize and industrialize products to create a better market for worldwide sales. Both of these factors, technology and a united market, are influencing the production of traditionally made food products. Yet there still exists a piece of the past that maintains itself in the art of a few food producers, some of whom belong to what may be a dying tradition.

Can we slow our lives down long enough to ponder the laborious task of collecting the rice that goes into our risotto, or long enough to imagine the thirty years it took to create the heavenly drop of balsamic vinegar we use to embellish a shard of Parmigiano-Reggiano cheese? Can we contemplate the day-to-day life of a man who hand-picks capers or one who fastidiously hand-dips chocolates? These are the people whose passion and dedication to their art will hopefully withstand the challenges of modern commerce. Our understanding of their work will help us appreciate what they add to our lives, especially when we compare it to the mass of industrial products competing for space on our table.

Italy's history and reputation for exceptional food runs deep. Reverence and ingenuity have led to practices of preparation and preservation that have changed little until the relatively recent introduction of machines and commercial transport. In a country politically united for just over a century, pride in regional foods remains strong. One can easily link a region with the food it produces: Emilia-Romagna's prosciutto, Parmigiano-Reggiano cheese, and balsamic vinegar; the olive oil of Liguria and Tuscany; Umbria's black truffles, Piedmont's white; Val d'Aosta's Fontina cheese and Lombardy's Gorgonzola; Tre Venezia's corn for polenta; pasta from Abruzzo; the seafood of coastal Marches; Molise's saffron; the abundant vegetables of Lazio; Campania's buffalo mozzarella and citrus; Apulia's wheat; the sun-dried figs and tomatoes of Calabria; Basilicata's *lucanica* sausage; Sicily's capers; and Sardinia's honey and pecorino cheese.

In the pages that follow, I will introduce you to the human faces behind some of Italy's most renowned food products, describe the techniques of producing them, and offer ways—recipes from the artisans, from Italian restaurateurs, and from my own kitchen—to prepare them. It is a culinary journey that changes region by region, yet consistently takes us toward a simpler life, focused on maintaining time-honored traditions.

# I

# *CONDIMENTS*

## OLIVE OIL
Family Mori

*Artisanal olive oil manufacturers*

## TRADITIONAL BALSAMIC VINEGAR
Francesco Renzi, *master cooper*
Giovanni Leonardi, *producer*

*A tale of two vinegars*

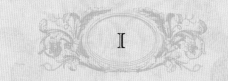

# I

*Balsamic vinegar ages in barrels made from a variety of aromatic woods.*

## CONDIMENTS

The olive and the grape are symbols of Italian cuisine. While olive oil and vinegar have many uses in the kitchen, they are also both essentials on the Italian dining table. Cold-pressed oils and carefully aged vinegars serve as the glorious finishing touch to many dishes.

Every fall excitement builds toward the moment when the olives will be picked and pressed. After days, perhaps weeks, of weather watching, Tuscan olives have ripened to perfection and are ready to be harvested. The first pressing is accompanied by a celebration using the oil in the purest way—grilled bread rubbed with garlic and dipped in the bright-green, peppery liquid.

In the past, olives were pressed without the benefit of machinery. Horses pulled heavy granite stones which ground the olives into a paste that was pressed, then transferred to huge ceramic urns, where it sat until the sediment settled and the water separated. Today, technology has updated the process, mechanically squeezing, filtering, and centrifuging the olives, while making sure they avoid contact with air and thus possible oxidation. Traditional olive oil mills are being forced to adopt these methods in order to stay competitive, yet strive for a happy medium that will enable them to maintain the quality of the product and survive the pressure of modern economy.

Balsamic vinegar, especially the traditional product that takes nearly half a lifetime to make, is most at home as a condiment—a drop at a time over meats, vegetables, fruits, or cheeses. It must be used discriminately and savored to the greatest possible degree. The laborious process for making it begins with fresh grapes, cooked to a thick, sweet consistency, then passed through barrels made of a variety of woods, often aging for thirty years or more. Stored in a light and airy attic, subject to the heat of summer and the cold of winter, it will age and thicken to the consistency of molasses.

The world is craving balsamic vinegar. Germany is the largest consumer, with the United States right behind. But there is a great deal of confusion in labeling and production between the artisanal product and competitive products of lower quality.

Every producer of balsamic vinegar whom I have met is an artisan, so choosing one person to write about was difficult. The commitment of time needed to make this superior product demands a true passion and unwavering patience. To make the choice more difficult, I had to decide whether to write about a producer who makes only traditional balsamic vinegar or one who also makes younger, nonconsortium versions (see A Tale of Two Vinegars, page 29). I support the work of the consortium and I respect the traditional condiment above all others, but I also like to cook with the vinegars that have been aged for a shorter time. I believe that in time there will be a legal designation for them. Meanwhile, I will continue to cook with them and use the aceto balsamico tradizionale in the manner intended, drop by precious drop.

Comparing industrial and artisanal versions of olive oil or balsamic vinegar is like putting a Fiat 500 next to a Lamborghini. They're both Italian, and they both have their places. You just have to decide which style suits your needs. Praise the traditional condiments. Such careful production deserves a place of honor at the table.

# OLIVE OIL
## Family Mori

### Loc. Palazzone, San Casciano dei Bagni (Tuscany)

*At the massive dining table, Filippo sits impatiently, jumping up every few minutes to rearrange the logs in the wood-burning oven. "Oh, the baby was teething on that," laughs Benedetta as she picks a piece of Parmigiano-Reggiano rind off the dark red brick floor. The dough for the pizza rests on an ancient piece of wood furniture that looks like an innocent chest of drawers. The simple toppings are standing by: home-cured olives, cheese, prosciutto, fresh herbs, end-of-the-season tomatoes. There, on the table, stands the ever-present bottle of olive oil, traditionally milled in a single cold pressing in the family* frantoio.

*Tenuta di Capezzana, Carmignano, fall 1993*

The autumn is a special time to be in Tuscany, from the grape harvest early in the season until the olives are picked and milled as winter approaches. The harmonious marriage of the region's climate, soil, excellent root stock, and tradition is evident in the extraordinary olive oil produced here, a quality due in large part to the cold climate. The olives are hand-picked in November, just before the weather dips below freezing. This timing is crucial. They must not be fully ripened if the oil is to be lively, herbal, and peppery— the characteristics of a good Tuscan oil. Life stands still as the exact moment of picking is decided. There is considerable study of the sky, with hands resting on hips. Will it rain? Will it freeze tonight?

The moment has arrived. Time is of the essence. All available hands are at work, even the children. Some of the pickers trade their labor for oil. The preferred method for picking is simply with the hands, wearing gloves to protect the harvester's arms from the scratchy branches. A small hand rake, or *pettino*, is also used to dislodge the olives, guiding them into the *bruscola*, a half-moon wicker basket strapped over the

*Mario Mori (at the head) and friends* a tavola.

shoulders and secured to the front of the picker's waist. Some olives fall into the nets spread below.

At eighty-seven, Lidia Mori doesn't go out to pick the olives anymore, but it doesn't mean she isn't working. In her kitchen, she prepares the meal for the hungry pickers who will soon return. On the wood fire— "always burning, year-round," she tells me—a large soup pot filled with beans and a local winter green called *cavolo nero* simmers.

A knobby loaf of bread cools on the front of the hearth, just in from the wood-fired oven outside. The kitchen has stories to tell. For two hundred years the Mori family has lived here in southern Tuscany, making wine and olive oil. Lidia's five children, now grown with families of their own, have scattered. Two sons still live nearby, however, and help her with the work of their 500-hectare (1,250-acre) farm. The second eldest, Mario, oversees the milling of the olives, and the youngest, Alberto, works on the business end. "Family is important, from our hearts, *proprio cuore*," Lidia says. "Tradition is important. We've always made oil this way."

Great tubs of olives, Frantoio, Moraiolo, and Leccino, await their turn at the mill, some shining

*Grinding the olives after harvest.*

down into tubs. The oil is filtered through a metal-screened wooden box, then poured into the large *orci*, classic terra-cotta urns with wide mouths, for natural decantation. As the oil rises, it is skimmed with a plate into another ceramic urn. The process is repeated four times, with standing time of twelve hours between skimming. Finally, almost all of the oil has been removed and the sediment has fallen to the bottom of the container. In the last separation, there still remains a questionable mix of oil and water. This is sent to the *inferno*, to "hell," a receptacle that holds the inferior oil mixture. In the past, it was used for lamp oil. Now it is carefully disposed of so as not to pollute the environment.

The oil that comes from this first pressing is called *polpa*, literally "pulp." This is the premium product, the condiment with the intense perfume of the olive that is drizzled over many typical Tuscan dishes, from soups to vegetables to meat. There is a secondary product as well. Once the fruit and pits have been ground and pressed for *polpa*, the paste is returned to the mill for another grinding and subsequent pressing in a mechanical device, the most modern piece of equipment in the *frantoio*: a 1920 Fiat press and pump. This second pressing is called *nocciola*, or "nut," an allusion to the pit of the olive, which continues to give up oil. The oil at this stage is still considered extra-virgin, although it is milder and is typically used for cooking.

"The *frantoio* is always a time and place for great socialization for the pickers and families," says

green and deep purple, others nearly black little orbs not much bigger than an almond. Before they have a chance to ferment, Mario removes twigs and debris and releases the olives evenly onto enormous millstones, the *macine*, round blocks of travertine that date back to 1900. As in the past, they are turned by the power of a horse. After an hour of grinding, the olives have become a coarse paste, which is then spread an inch thick onto the *fiscoli*, disks made of woven coconut fiber reinforced with nylon thread. Two to three hundred disks are used each season, made by hand over the rest of the year by a man in Foligno, an Umbrian town an hour away. Mario says, "He is the only artisan I know to still make *fiscoli* by hand. Now he is retired and only makes them for us. It worries me more every time I go to pick them up, because now he doesn't invoice us."

Once loaded, the disks are stacked, placed on the ancient wooden press, and slowly compressed, using leverage from long wooden beams to expel the liquid

Mario. "At the end of the season, we join all of the tables together for a *tavolata*, and everyone gathers to celebrate the new oil."

Lidia has joined Mario in the *frantoio*, adding wood to an old stone fireplace. She directs her son to place a grill on top, and puts some slices of her home-made bread to toast. Whole cloves of garlic are rubbed over the surface of the hot bread, releasing the aromatic scent, and some of the fresh oil is brought for dipping *bruschetta*, grilled Tuscan bread. This is the shining moment for the oil. With acidity well below one-half of a percent, the flavor explodes in the back of the throat—hot, green, peppery, addictive.

In the past, the Mori *frantoio* had two mill-stones operating, but now there is only one. With an annual harvest of roughly three hundred *quintale* (sixty thousand pounds) of olives, the family produces approximately ten thousand bottles of oil a year. Each

*The* bruscola *is strapped on the waist to gather olives.*

bottle, which holds five hundred milliliters (about sixteen ounces), is hand-dated and sold only locally. This is the art of extra-virgin olive oil, extracted without heat, chemicals, or filtration. "The fruit is important, but the quality is controlled by the man who makes the oil," insists Mario. "I watch the speed of the horse carefully. If he moves too fast, the friction will heat up the oil too much. I can tell by the number of times the wheel turns in a quarter hour." Once the olives start coming in, and the mill is up and running, the work usually continues for at least a month, twenty-four hours a day, with variations depending on the harvest and the weather. Naturally, the horse is changed every six hours, but it is essential to keep the process continuous so the olives don't have a chance to ferment before they are ground and pressed.

In the past, the Mori *frantoio* operated as a community mill. Now, only a few close friends and family still bring their olives for pressing their yearly supply of oil. The stone milling takes about a half hour, and the pressing about an hour or so. There is a little chair strapped onto the horse's harness, the *seggiolina*, to give the village children a ride while their fathers wait for the milling of their harvest.

"I have many pleasurable memories of this place," says Mario, smiling. "As a child I remember the warmth after a cold day of picking olives and the veil of night as we worked in the dark hours. Now I enjoy watching my children playing here, riding the *seggiolina*, and taking part in the tradition and slow pace of our old ways of oil making."

*Olive pulp is squeezed on an ancient wooden press.*

*Olive oil is the basis of much of Italian cooking, from the sautéing of the aromatic flavoring base called* soffritto, *a mixture of carrot, onion, and celery, to its use as an exquisite condiment drizzled over dishes at the table, often dubbed the "blessing."*

*Most contemporary olive oil producers use technology to increase their production. Yet a great number still respect traditional methods, hand-picking the olives and milling with a stone. Oils vary from region to region, from the peppery Tuscan condiments to the buttery oils of the south. Taste them all to see what you like. Most intense when first pressed, the flavor of the oil gradually mellows with time. Buy fresh oil, less than a year old for optimum flavor, and store it in a cool, dark place for no more than a year.*

*Some excellent producers whose oils are available in the United States are Avignonesi (Tuscany), Tenuta di Capezzana (Tuscany), Castello di Cacchiano (Tuscany), Castello di Ama (Tuscany), Bartolini (Umbria), Lungarotti (Umbria), Rustichella d'Abruzzo (Abruzzo), and Gardi "I Lecci" (Liguria).*

# BRUSCHETTA
*Grilled Bread with Olive Oil*

Traditionally, the first pressing of the olive harvest is tasted on the spot, drizzled over grilled bread. *Bruschetta* has become a popular restaurant item as well, served with a variety of toppings, from the traditional fresh tomato and basil to thin slices of sweet prosciutto and peppery arugula leaves. In every case, however, the freshest extra-virgin olive oil is used.

Grill or toast the bread slices on both sides. Remove from the heat and rub immediately on one side with the garlic cloves. Place on a platter, garlic side up, and drizzle with the olive oil. Serve at once.

SERVES 6

*1 loaf country-style bread, 1 pound, sliced ½ inch thick*

*4 whole cloves garlic, peeled*

*Extra-virgin olive oil, preferably freshly milled*

# PINZIMONIO
*Olive Oil Dip*

Much emphasis is put on seasonal vegetables in Italy, and at their peak they are sublime with nothing more than a simple dip of olive oil, especially if it is freshly milled.

*Spring and summer vegtables such as sugar snap peas, asparagus, baby carrots, fennel, and sweet bell peppers*

*or*

*Fall vegtables such as mushrooms, cardoons, potatoes, and beets*

*Extra-virgin olive oil for dipping*

*Salt and freshly ground pepper to taste*

@ Arrange an assortment of seasonal vegetables on a platter. Depending on the vegetables, you may first need to blanch or roast them. Let everything come to room temperature before serving.

@ Offer your guests small dishes of fruity extra-virgin olive oil for dipping and let them season it with salt and freshly ground pepper.

# BAGNA CAUDA
*Hot Olive Oil Sauce*

The name of this Piedmontese dipping sauce literally translates as "hot bath." Because it is a warm antipasto, the dish is seen more frequently in the cold-weather months, which also takes advantage of freshly milled olive oil. Serve the dip with raw or cooked vegetables. It is especially good with boiled potatoes and cardoons, a fall vegetable with the subtle hint of artichoke.

*½ cup extra-virgin olive oil*

*4 tablespoons unsalted butter*

*6 cloves garlic, minced*

*4 anchovy fillets*

@ In a small saucepan over low heat, combine the olive oil, butter, and garlic. Warm the mixture slowly for 10 minutes, allowing the oil to infuse with the flavor of the garlic, but do not allow the garlic to brown.

@ Add the anchovies, mashing them with a fork to blend them into the oil mixture. Heat through and transfer to a fondue pot or other vessel to keep the mixture warm while serving.

*SERVES 4*

# PANE SANTO

*Holy Bread* - Massimiliano Mariotti

This "holy bread" is so named because of the blessing of fresh olive oil drizzled over the top. Massimiliano Mariotti, executive chef at Fattoria Le Capezzine, the winery of Avignonesi in Montepulciano, makes this traditional Tuscan antipasto with *cavolo nero*, literally "black cabbage," a dark green, leafy vegetable grown in the fall. If you are unable to find it in your market, you can substitute kale, Swiss chard, or spinach and eliminate the initial boiling.

✎ Bring a saucepan of water to a boil. Add the *cavolo nero* and cook over medium-low heat until tender, about 1 hour. Drain, reserving the water.

✎ Prepare a fire in a grill, or preheat a broiler.

✎ In a sauté pan over medium heat, warm the 3 tablespoons olive oil. Add the *pancetta*, onion, minced garlic, and *peperoncino* and sauté until golden brown, 4 to 5 minutes. Raise the heat to medium-high, add the *cavolo nero*, and stir to blend well. Add the vinegar and continue to cook until some of the vinegar evaporates, 1 or 2 minutes more. Season with salt and pepper and keep warm.

✎ Toast the bread on the grill or in the broiler, turning once, until golden on both sides. Remove and rub both sides of each slice with the whole garlic clove. One half slice at a time, dip one side of the bread in the reserved cooking water, just enough to moisten the surface.

✎ Arrange the toast, dipped side up, on a tray and top with the *cavolo nero* mixture, dividing evenly. Garnish with a drizzle of olive oil and a sprinkling of freshly ground pepper.

*SERVES 6*

*12 cups julienned* cavolo nero

*3 tablespoons extra-virgin olive oil, plus extra oil for garnish*

*3 ounces* pancetta, *finely chopped*

*1 onion, finely chopped*

*1 clove garlic, minced, plus 1 whole clove*

*1 dried* peperoncino (red chile), *finely chopped*

*2 tablespoons red wine vinegar*

*Salt and freshly ground pepper to taste*

*6 slices country-style bread, cut in half*

# TORTA DI CAPEZZANA

*Olive Oil Cake* ~ Contessa Lisa Contini Bonacossi

Tenuta di Capezzana, the estate of Conte Ugo and Contessa Lisa Contini Bonacossi, stands in the gentle hills west of Florence, overlooking the Arno Valley. Documents dating back to 804, in the time of Charlemagne, note the production of wine and olive oil on the property, which were bartered in exchange for use of the land. Today Frantoio, Moraiolo, Pendolino, Leccino, and Santa Caterina olives are milled in a single cold pressing in the family *frantoio* for one of Tuscany's best artisanal oils.

      At Tenuta di Capezzana, if any of this moist rich cake is left over from dessert, it is finished off with *cappuccini* at the next day's breakfast.

*3 eggs*

*2½ cups granulated sugar*

*1½ cups extra-virgin olive oil*

*1½ cups milk*

*Grated zest of 3 oranges, plus 1 orange, sliced, for garnish*

*2 cups unbleached all-purpose flour*

*½ teaspoon baking powder*

*½ teaspoon baking soda*

*Pinch of salt*

*Confectioners' sugar for dusting*

&#8478; Preheat an oven to 350°F. Butter and flour a 12-inch cake pan.

&#8478; In a large bowl, whisk together the eggs and granulated sugar until blended. Add the olive oil, milk, and orange zest and mix well. In another bowl, stir together the flour, baking powder, baking soda, and salt. Add to the egg mixture, stirring just until blended. Do not overmix. Pour the batter into the prepared pan.

&#8478; Bake until a toothpick inserted into the center comes out clean, 50 to 55 minutes. Remove to a wire rack to cool completely. Loosen the sides with a knife and invert onto a serving plate.

&#8478; Dust the cake with confectioners' sugar and cut into 12 slices. Garnish the individual servings with fresh orange slices.

*SERVES 12*

# TRADITIONAL BALSAMIC VINEGAR
## Francesco Renzi, *master cooper,* Modena
## Giovanni Leonardi, *producer,* Magreta
### (Emilia-Romagna)

*I'm in the middle of a balsamic war. Not the kind of war where missiles are fired, but an emotional, historical, and political battle in which a journalist can make friends and foes with just a few words.*

*Modena, May 1998*

If you were to drive through the region of Emilia-Romagna only on the *autostrada*, your impression would be one of an endless landscape of farms dotted with industry. Centrally located north of Tuscany, south of the Dolomites, and ribboned with the Po River, the rich Padano plain is, in fact, a wealth of farmland and industry and home to two of Italy's largest agricultural producers, Parmalat and Barilla. But if you were to leave the high-speed route and take to the Via Emilia, the ancient road that connected Rome to the north, you would wander off on little side roads among rolling hills and vales of such beauty that you would begin to understand the passion of the local people for their territory.

Along with the abundance of the land, Emilia-Romagna is home to artists of all kinds. Names like Toscanini, Verdi, Pavarotti, and Ferrari are household words, found on street signs and hardware stores. The region is also the birthplace of some of Italy's most glorious foods: *prosciutto di Parma*, tortellini, Parmigiano-Reggiano cheese, and the precious condiment, balsamic vinegar.

The history of balsamic vinegar can be traced back to the eleventh century, when it was valued by the noble families for its healing properties. In fact, the word *balsamic* is probably derived from *balm*, a soothing

*Giovanni Leonardi.*

treatment. The process for making it is quite different than that for traditional vinegar. For the latter, wine is aged in bottles in a cool, dark cellar. Balsamic vinegar starts with sweet fresh grape must, which is cooked and reduced to an even sweeter consistency before being placed in wooden barrels and stored in airy attics to age. Until recently, it was only made for family use, with barrels that had been handed down for centuries, often part of a daughter's dowry.

As you travel in the area surrounding the towns of Modena and Reggio Emilia, you begin to consider the possibility that every innocent-looking farmhouse has a battery of barrels in their attic, many of them hundreds of years old. Chances are, many of the newer barrels are made by Francesco Renzi, master cooper in Modena.

Francesco can trace his family's roots back to the eleventh century in Bavaria. At the time, there was a great migration from present-day Germany south to what is now Italy, and the Renzi ancestors settled in the heavily wooded northern alpine area to "dedicate themselves to the arduous trades of woodsman and cooper." This tradition of crafting barrels in the German style stayed with the family as Francesco's namesake grandfather brought the business to Castelfranco Emilia,

*Francesco Renzi and his son hand-crafting a barrel.*

only part of Francesco's business. More than eight hundred thousand barrels, including wine barrels, are produced in this workshop each year, a stunning number considering the work is all done by hand.

The barrels for balsamic range in size from ten to seventy-five liters and are made from aromatic woods: oak, chestnut, acacia, ash, wild cherry, and the extremely rare juniper and mulberry. Each wood is handled differently, depending on its hardness. Usually a barrel is made entirely of only one wood, but occasionally Francesco will make one with two or three types of wood in the end caps. Recently he has been experimenting with apple, fig, and pear, but he thinks these woods may not be hard enough to stand the test of time. The wooden staves are extra thick, prepared by immersing them in boiling water and bending them by hand. They are placed under a press for three months, and then left to dry in the open air for four to five years. In mid-September, when the weather is humid, the wood is brought in and the barrels are built by hand. It is precise work, snugly fitting together the staves and binding them with metal rings, so that when the barrels go to work there will be no problems with leakage. Obviously, after a hundred years, barrels will begin to leak, but this seasoned wood is too dear to throw away. When the barrels need repair, a new barrel is fitted snugly around the old one, conserving generations of balsamic flavors. This important task requires as much craft as making a new barrel.

The Renzi family even has an *acetaia*, an attic where balsamic vinegar is aged. Francesco's pride is a battery of ten barrels of oak, ash, mulberry, cherry, and the highly prized juniper, all made by his ancestors. The larger barrels, which were originally used for

near Modena, in the early 1900s. The move to Modena took place in 1924, and the business continues to flourish there. From 1955 to 1978, Dionisio, Francesco's father, ran the operation. Francesco apprenticed with his father for twenty years before assuming management of the business in 1978, although his father still plays an active role. Now, Francesco's sons, Roberto and Matteo, carry on the family tradition, making wine and vinegar barrels daily alongside their father.

When I first met Francesco, he seemed a bit gruff. I could see he was a busy man, and he told me he could only spare an hour for our meeting. Grateful for that, I let him lead me through his operation in Modena. Several hours and a memorable lunch later, we were scheduling a visit for the next day as well. A craftsman and a perfectionist, the barrels for balsamic vinegar are wine and were brought from Germany by his great-grandfather, bear the name Rensi, a variant spelling of the family name from the Veneto in the 1800s.

After learning the history of the Renzi family, I was not surprised to see some very old barrels with Rensi stamped on them at an *acetaia* south of Modena, in Magreta. Here, near the Secchia River and the boundary dividing the provinces of Modena and Reggio Emilia, is the little farm of Giovanni Leonardi, dedicated to the production of balsamic vinegar. Visiting Leonardi is like stepping back in time. The dirt road leading into the farm winds through an assortment of chickens, peacocks, dogs, and cats. It looks as though all of the animals in the area have discovered their own little slice of heaven. Surrounded by grapevines, the farmhouse and *acetaia* were founded in the 1800s, their origins in the court of the Este family. Two buildings house the barrel collection in their attics. Below are the tools and work areas for the maintenance of the farm: the giant vats used to cook the grape must, a small tasting and sales area, and a room full of new barrels in preparation for use in balsamic vinegar production. In the fall, giant gourd-like squashes are suspended to dry for decorative purposes; in the past they were used as vessels to store the vinegar. Narrow wooden stairs are hung with an exposition of old tools from the farm and *acetaia*. The walls of every room are lined with antiques, not the least of which are the barrels. In addition to the Rensi barrels, there are also old barrels from Bologna and barrels with bands of hammered iron bearing the symbols of Mathilde, daughter of the noble Este family.

Upon entering the *acetaia*, a wonderful aroma wafts up to greet the visitor. In the dim light, one can see row upon row of barrels in graduating sizes. The three-inch opening in the top of each barrel is exposed to the air, covered only with a piece of linen, and the contents both suffer and enjoy the vagaries of the climate.

It takes a year just to prepare new barrels to hold vinegar. After rinsing them with boiling salted water and boiling wine vinegar, the barrels are filled with wine vinegar and left to cure for a year. They are then rinsed

again with wine vinegar and partially filled with cooked grape must to start the process of making traditional balsamic vinegar.

By law, only certain grapes can be used to make balsamic vinegar. Leonardi, like many producers, uses only the white Trebbiano, but Occhio di Gatta, Spergola, Lambrusco, and Berzemino are also permitted. Every fall, usually in early September after the wine harvest,

*Old wine barrels are now used to begin the aging of* aceto balsamico.

the grapes are picked. In an outside wooden stall, Giovanni slowly boils down the grape must in an open pot until it forms a caramel-like consistency. The temperature is controlled to allow evaporation and concentration, ultimately reducing the must to one-third of its original volume. As the must cools for a day in the cooking vat, it begins a natural malolactic fermentation. The must is then strained and transferred to large oak barrels for a few years to continue the process of fermentation before being transferred to the series of small barrels.

The battery, or series of barrels, numbers five, nine, twelve, or fifteen. Each battery contains an assortment of woods, and almost every batch spends

Aceto balsamico *aging in the Acetaia Leonardi.*

guarantees the products, which pass a rigorous tasting by a panel of experts. Two levels are permitted to be packaged in consortium bottles: the first takes at least twelve years of aging to meet the standards, and the *extravecchio*, extra old, often requires thirty years or more to meet the approval of the master tasters. One or two drops are all that is required to change the complexion of a simple grilled meat into something sublime.

Leonardi also makes balsamic vinegars that use the same method to start, cooking the grapes and aging them in wood, but are bottled after only five or ten years. These are wonderful added to cooked sauces or tossed with grilled vegetables.

a year in a barrel made of juniper, an intense and unique flavor. The barrels are kept in the farm's light-filled, airy attics, exposed to the climate, which is quite hot in the summer and cold in winter. Airborne yeasts enter as the vinegar is moved through the succession of barrels over a period of a minimum of twelve years. Each year a small amount is removed from the last, and smallest, barrel. Historically this was the supply needed for the year. The available space in the last barrel is then replaced with vinegar from the second barrel. This process continues until the open space is in the first, or largest, barrel. The new cooked must is introduced into that space. No barrel is ever emptied. As a result, the vinegar in the barrels is a blend of many years' harvests, dating back to when the barrels were started, and its consistency is as thick and viscous as honey.

The Leonardi *acetaia* produces a range of products made from cooked and aged must. The top of the line is the traditional balsamic vinegar. The *Consorzio Produttori di Aceto Balsamico Tradizionale di Modena*, the protective consortium for traditional *aceto balsamico*,

*Strawberries with balsamic vinegar.*

# SCALOPPINE DELL'OSTERIA
## Pork Scallops with Balsamic Vinegar - Acetaia Leonardi

The *osteria* is a casual place to dine. In the province of Modena, most *osterie* have *scaloppine* on the menu, usually veal, and the dish is almost always served with *aceto balsamico*. The Leonardis use pork and serve it with a side dish of potato puree or boiled vegetables. When cooking, use a good-quality balsamic vinegar of Modena, the industrial version. Try to find one that has spent some time in wood and has some cooked grape must in it. If you are using *aceto balsamico tradizionale*, skip the step where it is added to the pan. Instead, simply drizzle it over the finished *scaloppine*.

*1 pound boneless pork loin, sliced ¼ inch thick*

*Unbleached all-purpose flour for dredging*

*2 tablespoons unsalted butter*

*2 tablespoons extra-virgin olive oil*

*Salt and freshly ground pepper to taste*

*4 teaspoons* aceto balsamico di Modena

*1 cup beef or veal stock*

❦ One at a time, place the pork slices between two pieces of parchment paper and pound with a meat tenderizer until an even ⅛ inch thick. Dip lightly in the flour and shake off the excess.

❦ In a large sauté pan over medium heat, melt the butter with the oil. Add the pork slices and brown, turning once, on both sides. Season with salt and pepper. Add the *aceto balsamico* and cook until reduced slightly, 3 to 4 minutes. Remove the pork to a warmed platter and keep warm.

❦ Add the stock to the pan, ¼ cup at a time, reducing for 3 to 4 minutes after each addition until thickened. Spoon the sauce over the *scaloppine* and serve at once.

*SERVES 4*

# FRAGOLE CON ACETO BALSAMICO
## Strawberries with Balsamic Vinegar

In the early spring, tiny wild strawberries pop up along the banks of the Secchia River. According to Clara Leonardi, Giovanni's daughter, the berries are absolutely heavenly simply sprinkled with *aceto balsamico tradizionale* or with their *Patriarca dei Balsamici*, a condiment of cooked must that has been aged ten years in wood.

**For each person:**

*½ cup strawberries, hulled and left whole or sliced*

*1 teaspoon* aceto balsamico tradizionale

❦ Place the strawberries in a nonreactive bowl. Drizzle with the balsamic vinegar and let stand for about 5 minutes, then serve in cups.

# FRITTATA RUSTICA

*Potato Frittata with Balsamic Vinegar* - Moreno Giusti

The Leonardis have forged an alliance with chef Moreno Giusti of Ferrara, who proposes that certain foods have a seductive quality, especially heady aged balsamic vinegar. In any case, eggs are the perfect medium to experience the richness and perhaps, as the chef suggests, the sensual attributes of traditional balsamic vinegar.

In a bowl, whisk together the eggs and Parmigiano-Reggiano cheese. Season with the nutmeg, salt, and pepper and set aside.

In a 10-inch sauté pan over medium-high heat, warm the olive oil. Add the onion and lemon zest and sauté until golden brown, 3 to 4 minutes. Deglaze the pan with the 2 teaspoons balsamic vinegar, loosening the browned bits from the surface of the pan. Add the potatoes and white wine and cook until reduced, 3 to 4 minutes.

Add the egg mixture, reduce the heat to medium, cover, and cook until the eggs have begun to set, 3 to 5 minutes. Sprinkle with the tomato dice, cover, and cook until the eggs are firm and the bottom is golden brown, about 2 minutes longer.

Loosen the edges and invert onto a large plate. Invert again onto a platter so that the tomatoes are on top. Cut into fourths. Drizzle with *aceto balsamico tradizionale* and serve at once.

SERVES 4

6 eggs

¼ cup grated Parmigiano-Reggiano cheese

Freshly grated nutmeg to taste

Salt and freshly ground pepper to taste

3 tablespoons extra-virgin olive oil

1 onion, coarsely chopped

1 lemon zest strip, 2 inches wide

2 teaspoons 15-year-old balsamic vinegar

2 potatoes, boiled until tender, peeled, and diced

¼ cup dry white wine

2 ripe tomatoes, peeled, seeded, and diced

aceto balsamico tradizionale

# A TALE OF TWO VINEGARS

*Since 1986, the traditional condiment,* aceto balsamico tradizionale di Modena *or* aceto balsamico tradizionale di Reggio Emilia, *has been protected by law, with both the methods for making it and the ingredients carefully defined and permitted only in the provinces of Modena and Reggio Emilia. The product is painstakingly evaluated and guaranteed by a consortium in each province. When you buy a bottle with the consortium seal, you know that the contents include only the must, pulp, from local grapes of specific varieties. The must will have been cooked over an open flame until reduced, and then aged in barrels of a variety of different woods for at least twelve years.*

*Also permitted by law is a product called* aceto balsamico di Modena. *By regulation, this vinegar, generically called* industriale, *is permitted to include wine vinegar and other ingredients such as caramel color and flavoring. It does not have the restriction of aging in wood for any period of time, and it doesn't have to contain any cooked must. In fact,* aceto balsamico di Modena *can be made with nothing more than wine vinegar combined with the above mentioned additives and put directly into a bottle. It is the product we see on supermarket shelves, often no more than a sweetened wine vinegar. While starting with cooked grapes and aging in wood isn't a legal requirement, there are still some producers who use at least a portion of cooked must and let it age a short time in wood. The best way for a consumer to determine what they are buying is to read the list of ingredients on the bottle.*

*The range of products available for purchase is astounding, some sensational, some wretched. Yet, they all bear the name* aceto balsamico di Modena. *It is a world apart from its traditional namesake,* aceto balsamico tradizionale.

*The two vinegars are used in completely different ways. The traditional product is strictly a condiment, served at the table to embellish a finished food. You should never cook a traditional balsamic vinegar. On the other hand, the industrial product can be used for salad.*

*In between these two outrageously different products are some vinegars that are made in the fashion of the traditional, but not aged as long. As a cook, I prefer to use them over any industrial balsamic vinegar. They start with cooked grape must, and they are aged in a variety of woods for three or five or ten years. They cost less than the traditional vinegar, but there really is no comparison. These "in-between" vinegars would never meet the consortium's minimum qualifications in a tasting. Therefore they cannot be sold as a traditional condiment, yet they are much more than an industrial product. But, here is the rub: there is no legal recognition for something that is neither traditional nor industrial. A battle is currently ensuing in Modena between the consortium and the people who are making vinegars similar to traditional, but not consortium approved. It is a worthwhile struggle on the part of the consortium, for there are many counterfeit vinegars claiming to be "traditional."*

# II

## *BREAD*

**MILLER**
Giuseppe Parigi

**BREAD BAKER**
Giuseppe di Gesù

*The famous bread of Altamura.*

# BREAD

Today bread is found on every Italian table, but before World War II white flour was primarily for the upper classes. What the lower classes could afford was often a dark, dense bread made with more economical grains and baked in community ovens. Shortly after the war, large industry stepped in and began to supply an insipid, characterless white bread. In a country that demands taste, a revival of traditional loaves was inevitable, however, and it happened in the seventies. Italy boasts over thirty-five thousand ovens now, most of them small community bakeries supplying the local people with the regional breads of the area.

Some bakers estimate that Italy can claim over a thousand national breads, with each region contributing its own unique style, each very different from another. Only in Lombardy can you taste michetta, *in Piedmont* biova, *or in the Veneto* ciopa. *Some breads have become universal, of course, such as the traditional large, thick-crusted* pane casareccio *(homemade bread) and focaccia, but even the latter maintains its regional character with local toppings. But ask any Italian to name a famous regional bread, and he or she is likely to answer Altamura, a butter-yellow loaf made with local hard-wheat flour in the charming Apulian town of the same name. The bread has a longer-than-average shelf life, and it is not difficult to imagine it as one of the foods packed for the historical* transumanza, *the migration in the spring and fall of shepherds and their herds. This traditional path, which is still visible in some areas, began in Abruzzo and ended in Foggia, the area where much of Apulia's wheat is grown.*

Bread baking in Italy, however, stretches back to long before the first transumanza. *Although certainly the ancient Romans were making flat breads of crushed grains and baking them on hearthstones, the art of leavened bread may have come from ancient Greece, from which conquering Romans brought back cooks and bakers to their capital. In the third century* B.C., *the Romans outfitted their clay ovens with water vessels to introduce steam for a crispier crust. Three centuries later, Roman architect Vitruvius designed and built a water-powered mill that could adjust the coarseness or fineness of the flour, a feature that led to many new bread styles. In 25* B.C., *a horse-powered mill came into use in Rome. Not long after that the same mechanism was used to mix doughs.*

A water-driven mill is an uncommon sight these days. I first learned about the one in the Tuscan village of Loro Ciuffenna from wine and food expert Burton Anderson, author of Treasures of the Italian Table. *Burton describes Giuseppe Parigi's battle with health officials to modernize and sanitize his ancient mill. Fortunately, Parigi found sanctuary under the aegis of* Belle Arti, *the association that protects architectural monuments and other treasures.*

Also part of Italian bread history are the superstitions and proverbs that equal the number of different breads sold in the country's bakeries. In Carol Field's book, The Italian Baker, *she describes the Apulian legend that condemned anyone who wasted bread crumbs to purgatory for the same number of years as the number of crumbs that were left. To avoid a similar fate, toss your leftover bread crumbs with a little olive oil and spread them on a baking sheet to toast, then sprinkle them over pasta or vegetables.*

# MILLER
## Giuseppe Parigi
### Loro Ciuffenna (Tuscany)

*Nothing prepared me for the beauty of the rushing river and the ancient mill at its side. You can see the waterwheels, the* ritrecene, *turning in the current. There is a Tuscan quip about a person who is "going ritrecene"—it means someone who is talking nonstop.*

*Loro Ciuffenna, May 1997*

Market day in Loro Ciuffenna is Monday. The village's only public parking lot is filled with the ten or twelve vendors selling wares from vegetables to espresso makers to shampoo. This microcosm of daily life, replete with plastic colanders, aprons, and freshly picked porcini, is set against the magnificent backdrop of the Ciuffenna River, tumbling and roaring over large rocks in its mad rush to meet the Arno. Settled into the side of the riverbank, just above the bridge, is a building that dates back to the 1100s. Visible from the other side of the river are the workings of the mill that it houses. Powered by the river, paddled waterwheels, *ritrecene,* drive the millstone that grinds the grains as it has done for centuries. Since 1958, it has been the daily work of Giuseppe "Beppe" Parigi, who inherited it from his wife's family.

Beppe has three working millstones, with a waterwheel to power each. A wooden lever operates the chute that lets the water enter the space beneath the floor where the wheel waits. Within seconds, the wheel begins to turn the wooden screw that rotates the stone. The sound of the water below, the creaking wood of the mechanisms, and the grinding of the stone are all *simpatico* with the natural setting, as

*Beppe Parigi.*

is Beppe. "The working parts are replaced every hundred years or so," he says quietly without looking up, the perpetual cigarette dangling from his flour-dusted face as he pours grains from burlap bags into the chute. He only mills "tender" grains such as the soft local wheat or corn. From November to February, chestnuts are in season, the flour a dusky tan with a positively nutty aroma. The flour passes to the *buratto,* a screened cylinder encased in wood that rotates to filter and separate the bran and chaff, then is scooped into large brown paper bags to sell. Some of the farmers *pagare natura,* "pay in nature," leaving a portion of their flour in payment for the mill's work, but Beppe purchases most of the grains and mills them for sale. He delivers the bulk of his output to two bakeries in Florence, operations willing to pay extra for his hand-milled product, and the rest is sold to customers who come from all over the nearby countryside.

The days are long. "You just keep working until you get to 'dark time,' or until the work is done," says Beppe. "There is a miller's saying, 'When there is water, I can drink wine. When there is no water, I must drink water.'"

# CRESPELLE DI CASTAGNE
*Chestnut Crepes*

Triple chestnut! Chestnut flour in the crepes, chestnut puree in the filling, and musky chestnut honey drizzled on top. If fresh chestnuts are unavailable, use 12 ounces canned whole or pureed chestnuts.

**For the filling:**

*1 pound chestnuts*

*8 ounces (about 1 cup) mascarpone
   or ricotta cheese*

*¼ cup sugar*

*1 teaspoon vanilla extract*

**For the crepes:**

*½ cup chestnut flour*

*½ cup unbleached all-purpose flour*

*2 tablespoons sugar*

*1 cup milk*

*3 eggs*

*2 tablespoons unsalted butter, melted,
   plus melted butter for cooking*

*Chestnut honey to taste*

@ Preheat an oven to 375°F.

@ To make the filling, using a sharp knife, score the chestnuts with an X. In a large saucepan, combine the chestnuts with water to cover, bring to a boil, and boil for 5 minutes, then remove from the heat. When just cool enough to handle, remove from the water one at a time and peel away the hard outer shell and the "furry" layer beneath. (The nuts are easier to peel when hot, so leave them in the water until you are ready to peel them.) Place the peeled chestnuts on a baking sheet and roast in the oven until light golden brown, 12 to 15 minutes. Do not leave them in the oven too long, or they will be bitter. Remove and let cool.

@ In a food processor, combine the cooled chestnuts, cheese, sugar, and vanilla. Puree to a smooth consistency. Cover and chill until ready to use.

@ To make the crepes, in a blender, combine the flours, sugar, milk, eggs, and the 2 tablespoons melted butter. Process to form a smooth batter. Cover and chill for at least 1 hour or as long as overnight.

@ Heat a 6-inch nonstick skillet over medium heat. When hot, brush the pan with melted butter. Stir the batter, scoop out ¼ cup, and pour it into the pan. Tilt the pan so that the batter runs to the edges, creating a thin, even layer. Immediately loosen the edges with a spatula and cook until the top is set and looks dry, about 1 minute. Turn and cook until just lightly browned on the second side, 15 to 30 seconds.

@ Remove from the pan and repeat with the remaining batter, stacking the crepes with parchment paper between them as they are cooked. You should have 12 crepes in all. Keep at room temperature for up to 2 hours. The crepes can also be refrigerated for several hours. Bring them to room temperature before assembling.

@ To serve, place a spoonful of filling on each crepe and fold or roll to desired shape. Place on a serving platter and drizzle with chestnut honey.

*SERVES 4*

# CASTAGNACCIO

*Chestnut Cake* ~ Nancy Anderson

My friend Nancy Anderson, who has lived in Tuscany for twenty years, gave me her recipe for this dessert, a traditional Tuscan favorite. It is not, however, a dessert for everyone. It is quite dense and made without sugar because of the natural sweetness of the chestnut flour. A little sugar can be added to customize it for non-Tuscan palates. I've also added a topping of ricotta sweetened with a rosemary-infused chestnut honey.

◈ Preheat an oven to 475°F. Butter an 11-inch cake pan and dust it with bread crumbs.

◈ In a large bowl, combine the chestnut flour with a little of the water to make a smooth paste, then add the rest of the water, mixing well to obtain a creamy liquid. Add the sugar, if using, and the salt. Stir in the olive oil, pine nuts, walnuts, and the drained raisins. Pour into the prepared cake pan. Sprinkle the rosemary leaves over the top of the batter and drizzle with olive oil.

◈ Bake until golden and crisp on top, 35 to 40 minutes. The center will be moist and pudding-like. Remove to a wire rack to cool completely, then transfer to a serving plate.

◈ In a heatproof bowl placed over a saucepan of simmering water, warm the honey. Add the rosemary sprigs and remove from the heat. Let stand for at least 30 minutes or as long as 24 hours, then remove the sprigs.

◈ Slice the cake and place on individual plates. Top each serving with 2 tablespoons of ricotta cheese and drizzle with the rosemary-infused honey.

*SERVES 8*

Fine dried bread crumbs for dusting pan

3 cups sifted chestnut flour

2 cups water

½ cup sugar (optional)

Pinch of salt

5 tablespoons extra-virgin olive oil

¼ cup pine nuts, toasted

¼ cup crushed walnuts

3 tablespoons raisins, soaked in 3 tablespoons warm water

1 tablespoon fresh rosemary leaves, plus 3 sprigs

Extra-virgin olive oil for drizzling

1 cup chestnut honey

8 ounces (about 1 cup) ricotta cheese

# POLENTA

In a tiny room next to the mill, Beppe sells his flours along with some seeds and whole grains. He mills oats, barley, and corn to different consistencies for animal feed, and also finely grinds corn to make a silky polenta. You can substitute cornmeal for the polenta in this recipe.

*2 tablespoons olive oil*

*½ cup chopped onion*

*4½ cups chicken stock*

*1½ cups polenta*

*¼ cup grated Parmigiano-Reggiano cheese*

*Salt and freshly ground pepper to taste*

❧ In a large sauté pan over medium-high heat, warm the olive oil. Add the onion and sauté until golden brown, 3 to 4 minutes. Add the chicken stock and bring to a boil. Add the polenta slowly, whisking constantly. Reduce the heat to medium and continue to cook, stirring constantly, until the polenta easily comes away from the sides of the pot, 25 to 30 minutes.

❧ Stir in the Parmigiano-Reggiano cheese and season with salt and pepper. Remove to a warmed serving dish and serve at once.

*SERVES 4*

# BREAD BAKER
## Giuseppe di Gesù
### Altamura (Apulia)

*I was last in Apulia in 1983. The things that stick in my mind from that visit are the seafood and the time when I rear-ended a guy in Bari who just wasn't moving fast enough! And Alberobello with its curious cone-roofed stone buildings called* trulli—*they looked like they were from another world. This time I've come back to find the famous bread of Altamura.*

*Altamura, June 1998*

The bread of Altamura has a countrywide reputation. This clean, civilized town falls nearly in the center of the coastal region of Apulia, best identified as the heel of the Italian boot. The interior flatlands contribute an abundance of produce, in particular seas of hard durum wheat from the Tavoliere plain that surrounds the town of Foggia.

Bread is simply flour, leavening, water, and salt. So what gives the bread of Altamura its epic esteem? Baker Giuseppe "Beppe" di Gesù believes it is a combination of things. It starts with the *grano duro*, Apulia's hard durum wheat (*Triticum durum*), which is coarsely milled. This butter-yellow flour, also called *semola* (semolina), is tough with protein, a quality necessary to develop gluten for an elastic dough. Gluten is what gives the dough the structure to rise when the leavening releases its gases. Beppe's family uses a *lievito madre*, a "mother" that has been active since the time when his great-grandfather and grandfather operated Altamura's community ovens. "The yeast is the *anima,* the spirit of the dough," says Beppe. The mother regenerates itself daily with the unique airborne yeasts of Altamura; once the day's dough is made, a portion is left to stand overnight. The mixing bowl is never empty.

*Beppe di Gesù.*

Beppe started working with his father, Pasquale, and three uncles in his early teens. He took some courses in business management and a professional course in *Arte Bianca,* the bakery industry name for products that use flour. These educational programs helped him strengthen his business skills, but the true art of bread making came from his family's traditions. He learned that environment is a major contributor to the success of the bread—the little hills that hold the dry air, the local semolina, the airborne microorganisms—but perhaps the most surprising element is the water brought from the Naples countryside. According to Beppe, it is transported by a remarkable aqueduct system to Apulia, where it serves as tap water, rich in minerals and salt. The last ingredient in the bread is sea salt. In *Flavors of Puglia,* Nancy Harmon Jenkins describes how bakers in Bari used seawater during those times when the government imposed an extremely high salt tax.

Finally, this exceptional bread is also the result of the technique of the local bakers. The knowledge of how to handle dough and how to bake it comes from generations of experience. Beppe gives his bread three risings, for a total of eight hours, and then hand kneads it into over two hundred

*The di Gesù family bakers.*

the ashes are swept away and the oven is filled to capacity. The door is closed to conserve the heat for about thirty-five minutes, or until the expert bakers sense the time is right. Then the door is left ajar for another hour and ten minutes. Finally, the door is swung open, and the mounds of over 250 finished breads appear. One man works on the left side of the opening, one on the right. In a well-practiced choreography of motion, the bread is pulled from the dusky red glow of the oven on a long-handled peel. The ashes are brushed off, and the hot bread is transferred with bare hands to a flour-dusted *tavola*. With little effort, the effect is a piece of art. The size of each loaf ranges from a half kilo to two kilos (about one pound to almost four and a half pounds), but for special occasions they will make some that weigh six kilos (over thirteen pounds).

For the last twenty years, the four sons of the eldest Giuseppe have run the bakery. These days, their sons, Beppe and his cousins, are learning the secrets of the master bakers of Altamura.

---

*Meglio pane asciutto in casa propria che arrosto in casa di'altri.*

"Better to have stale bread in your house than roasted meat in someone else's house."—Italian proverb

---

pounds of loaves a day, destined for baking in one of the three ovens. Two of them are modern and one is the ancient wood-burning oven that dates back to Beppe's great-grandfather's time. Beppe remembers his father's stories about the time during the war when women would arrive at the crack of dawn to bring their loaves for baking. Brands for each family, which hung on the wall, were used to mark the breads for identification. Finished loaves were loaded on a *tavola* (a long, narrow board), and delivered by a *garzone,* a boy on a bicycle who called out "*pane*" as he made his rounds. Even now, two or three women a week bring their dough for baking. They often buy their *madre* from Beppe the day before and then rise at four o'clock to start making the dough. The brands are no longer used, but a razor mark identifies the loaves that will be picked up later in the day, warm and crusty from the wood-fired oven.

This ancient oven, rebuilt and reinforced fifty years ago, is fired up daily. The interior is made of stone and brick with a baking surface of *mazzero,* a stone that tolerates high temperatures.

Perhaps the fuel gives this bread its exceptional essence. While olive and almond wood are readily available in Apulia, Beppe says they are too hot and "violent." He prefers to start with a slow but intense fire made from small pieces of hardwood such as oak. The oven is constantly fed until it reaches a temperature of 575°F, then

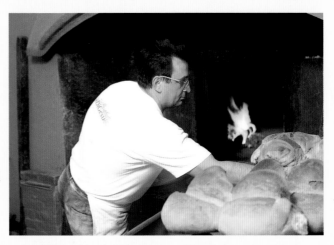

*The wood-burning oven has been used by four generations of bakers.*

# LIEVITO MADRE
*Natural Leavening* - Beppe di Gesù

According to Beppe di Gesù, this "mother" can be used as a starter after four hours of resting, provided it has been "kept in a baker's drawer with a cloth over it." It can be refrigerated for up to a week between uses as long as you continue to "feed" it with flour and water. Bakers in Italy use *lievito di birra*, a "beer" yeast. You can approximate it with a fresh yeast cake, usually found in health-food stores or gourmet markets.

*3½ cups semolina flour*
*2 cups warm water*
*½ ounce fresh yeast cake*

In a large bowl, with a wooden spoon, combine the flour, water, and yeast. Turn onto a lightly floured work surface and knead until smooth. Transfer to a large, lightly oiled bowl, cover with a towel, and let rise in a warm place for 4 hours.

Remove half of the dough for the bread you are about to make. Refresh the remaining dough for the next use with 1¾ cups (14 ounces) flour and 1 cup water, then knead on a floured work surface until smooth. Transfer to a large, lightly oiled bowl, cover, and refrigerate until ready to use.

*MAKES APPROXIMATELY 2 POUNDS*

# FOCACCIA ALLE OLIVE E POMODORI

*Flat Bread with Olives and Tomatoes* ~ Beppe di Gesù

Beppe warns that each time you knead the dough, you must let it rest. "It is like the human body . . . when you 'harm' it, it needs to rest to make it better."

℘ Place the flour on a work surface and make a well in the center. In a bowl, stir the yeast into 1 cup of the warm water and let stand until foamy on top, about 5 minutes. Pour the yeast mixture into the well in the flour. Mix the salt in the remaining 1 ½ cups warm water and add it to the well. With your fingers, begin to work the liquid into the flour. When the mixture forms a soft dough, add the *madre* and knead until smooth and elastic, 10 to 15 minutes. Cover with a towel and let rest in a warm place for 1 hour.

℘ Lightly oil 2 baking sheets. Knead the dough until smooth, about 10 minutes. Divide the dough in half and shape into two round disks, each about 10 inches in diameter and 1 inch thick. Place them on the prepared sheet pans and let rest for 30 minutes.

℘ Dimple the surface of each round with your fingertips, making impressions about ¼ inch deep. Scatter the tomatoes and olives on top, distributing them evenly over the surface. Sprinkle with coarse salt and the oregano, drizzle with olive oil, and let rest for 30 minutes. Meanwhile, preheat an oven to 425°F.

℘ Bake until golden brown, about 30 minutes. Serve at once.

*MAKES TWO 10-INCH ROUNDS*

*4 cups semolina flour*

*½ ounce fresh yeast cake*

*2 ½ cups warm water*

*1 tablespoon salt*

*½ recipe* Lievito Madre *(page 43)*

*2 firm, ripe tomatoes, cut into narrow wedges*

*20 to 25 Mediterranean-style oil-cured black olives*

*Coarse sea salt for sprinkling*

*1 tablespoon minced fresh oregano*

*Extra-virgin olive oil for drizzling*

# GRISSINI DI SEMOLINA
*Semolina Breadsticks*

Semolina flour gives baked goods a cracker-like texture. Always use a finely milled flour. I like Bob's Red Mill Semolina for Pasta, which is found in health-food stores. Semolina is really too tough for fresh pasta; it should be reserved for dried pastas and yeast doughs. Serve these crispy treats with salads, soups, or wrapped with prosciutto for an appetizer.

*3 cups semolina flour*

*½ ounce fresh yeast cake*

*1¼ cups warm water*

*1 tablespoon sugar*

*1½ teaspoons salt*

*¼ cup extra-virgin olive oil*

*Cornmeal for dusting*

❧ Place the semolina on a work surface and make a well in the center. In a small bowl, combine the yeast, ½ cup of the warm water, and the sugar. Let stand until foamy on top, about 5 minutes. Pour the yeast mixture into the well in the flour. In the same bowl, mix together the salt, the remaining ¾ cup warm water, and the olive oil, and add it to the well. With your fingers, begin to work the liquid into the flour. When the mixture comes together in a bowl, knead on a floured work surface until smooth and elastic, 10 to 15 minutes. Shape the dough into a rectangle about 6 inches wide, 15 inches long, and ½ inch thick. Place on a floured surface, cover with a towel, and let rest in a warm place for 1 hour.

❧ Meanwhile, place a baking stone in an oven and preheat to 450°F.

❧ Sprinkle a pizza peel with cornmeal. Dip a sharp knife into flour and cut the rectangle crosswise into 24 pieces. Shape each piece into a breadstick by gently rolling and stretching it on a lightly floured work surface until it is about 12 inches long. Place the stretched breadsticks on the pizza peel as you work.

❧ Slide the breadsticks onto the preheated baking stone and bake until golden brown, 15 to 20 minutes. Serve at once or remove to a wire rack to cool to room temperature.

*MAKES 2 DOZEN BREADSTICKS*

# III

## *CHEESE*

### CACIOCAVALLO
Mario Gallo and Francesco d'Elia

### MOZZARELLA DI BUFALA
Cecilia Baratta Bellelli, *buffalo milk producer*
Casearia Barlotti, *cheese cooperative*

*Typical regional cheeses*

### PARMIGIANO-REGGIANO
Luciano Catellani, *president of CVPARR*
Nello Faroni, *cheese maker*

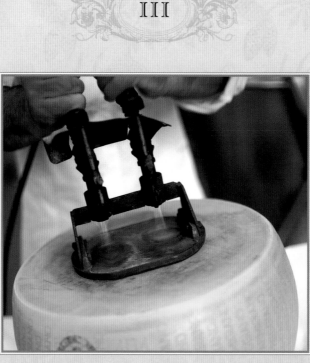

*Parmigiano-Reggiano cheese is branded with the logo of the red cow.*

# CHEESE

Italy's cheese traditions were born from the need to preserve milk and keep a source of available protein for workers, for travelers, and for the winter food supply. Milk of the cow, water buffalo, sheep, and goat has contributed to the wealth of over four hundred cheeses that can be found from the northern alpine regions to the toe of the boot and the islands. It was difficult, indeed, to single out what to write about here. I chose three of my favorites: caciocavallo, mozzarella di bufala, *and* Parmigiano-Reggiano. I wish I could have included more: Castelmagno, robiola di Roccaverano, pecorino, *and* Gorgonzola, *for example. Or* Asiago, Bra, provolone, *and* montasio. *And then there are* Fontina, Taleggio, *and* ricotta. *You can see the problem.*

Since 1955, Italian law has provided DOC (denominazione di origine controllata) *protection for many of the unique regional cheeses. This ruling is specific to the locale and the traditional process of making the cheese, and is often enforced and guaranteed by a consortium of producers. But even within* that legal definition, there is the possibility of a range of products, especially when an industrial counterpart is introduced. It is conceivable that, given the new standards for sanitation in the European market, most of us will never have the chance to taste some of the artisanal products I am describing here, unless you are in Italy, and even then, they are getting harder to find.

Parmigiano-Reggiano is a cheese that has been made according to the same traditions for seven hundred years. It remains one of the most wonderful-tasting cheeses I know, universally popular in Italy and all over the world. I remember the taste of a Parmigiano-Reggiano that I had fifteen years ago on my first trip to Italy. I stopped at a tiny dairy in Villa Cella, on the via Emilia, and walked through the brining and aging rooms. I tasted something there that I'll never forget—an amber shard from a freshly opened wheel. The moment it touched my tongue, I knew there was no equal to the King of Cheeses. It was full-bodied, rich, unctuous, yet firm. And it seemed to sizzle in my mouth as I savored it, an effect I learned later is due to the crystals the amino acids form as the cheese ages. It is a taste that I am searching for today, and I think I've found it in a cheese dairy in Cavriago.

I have nothing but good things to say about the consorzio that protects the quality of Parmigiano-Reggiano. They do an extraordinary job of guaranteeing that every wheel produced and branded by them is first quality, and their marketing programs have carried the product with great success to faraway lands.

But with big business comes standardization. More and more dairies are forming cooperatives, and the independent dairyman–cheese maker is becoming rare. With the disappearance of the individual artisan goes some of the distinct differences evident in the past, such as floral qualities in a mountain spring cheese, or the rich, pungent character in a plains-produced autumn cheese. Thanks to artificial insemination, dairies produce milk year-round, and because of controls on the feed, the cows are on similar diets.

Variations persist, however. Indeed, it would be impossible to standardize this artisanal product completely, for it is still influenced by the hand of the cheese maker. Imagine my pleasure when I found a stunning example of this: a consortium-approved Parmigiano-Reggiano made with the milk of an ancient breed of cows, a milk with enough protein to let it age a full year and a half longer than the others. It was the taste for which I was looking.

Pasta filata is the name for cheeses made by the process of cooking the curds in boiling water, tearing the mass into strips, and then shaping it by stretching or kneading. Among the well-known cheeses made this way are mozzarella, caciocavallo, scamorza, and provolone. In looking for the best mozzarella di bufala, I went straight to the source, a farm that raises water buffalo. Cecilia Baratta Bellelli was a gracious hostess, her long table laden with her estate's olive oil, wine, fruit, and vegetables. I am most grateful for her offer to drive me up into the mountains to see a cheese-making miracle: caciocavallo made today as it has been made throughout history.

# CACIOCAVALLO
## Mario Gallo
## Francesco d'Elia
### Cilento Mountains (Campania)

*It took us three hours of negotiating the rocky, mountainous dirt road ravaged by last winter's storms, winding around yet another corner that appeared to lead to the end of the world. Up past alpine meadows sprinkled with flowers, past stony hillsides dotted with scrub and corbezzolo bush, the source of bitter honey. When our four-wheel-drive vehicle finally gave out, Cecilia put on her hiking boots and we took a short walk back in time.*

*Cilento Mountains, June 1998*

A three-hour drive and several lifetimes above the lowlands surrounding Paestum, a slice of history endures. High in the Cilento Mountains, Francesco d'Elia, his sister Maria, and her husband, Mario Gallo, live the simplest of lives. For many years, Francesco and Mario have made the daily trek from their cottage to the meadows where their herd of about one hundred large, white Poldolica cows graze. Their shelter is an embrace of trees, worn with the living of many years, useful items hanging from every available notched branch. Life here is quiet and humble, with no electricity, no modern amenities. Most days are spent tending the cows, but in June work turns to the making of caciocavallo cheese. A wood fire burns all the day, nurtured by Maria, yielding at necessary intervals coffee, soup, and the boiling water needed to make the cheese.

No sounds of modern life reach this sanctum. The work is performed to a chorus of cowbells punctuated by an occasional call from a cuckoo. Behind these sounds is the percussion of fresh spring water running clear and bright into a retired copper pot blackened by years of cooking. Deep in the cool water rests the day's work,

*Francesco d'Elia shapes the caciocavallo by hand.*

the alabaster-white, pear-shaped cheese that will later hang over one of the tree branches. *Caciocavallo* literally means "cheese on horseback," named because the forms are tied in pairs and hung over a piece of wood (the *cavallo*, or horse) to age.

One of southern Italy's classic cheeses, caciocavallo is a *pasta filata*, that is, a cheese made by stretching and shaping by hand. Found in Campania, Basilicata, Molise, Apulia, and Calabria, it is believed by some sources to date back to the fourteenth century, at which time it may have been made from mare's milk. Today's caciocavallo comes from cow's milk and has a sweet, slightly salty flavor and a firm, smooth texture when fresh, but it is often aged from two months to two years. As it ages, its flavor becomes richer and its texture more granular, making it ideal for grating.

The milk is collected in the early morning. Like clockwork, the cows wander in from their meadows of sweet grasses and clover sprinkled with subalpine flowers, to yield a milk so rich that Maria often makes butter from the ricotta, the creamy cheese made by recooking the whey, a by-product of the caciocavallo.

It takes ten liters (about ten quarts) of milk and three to four hours of work, depending on the weather, to make one cheese.

Maria heats the fresh milk over the wood fire and curdles it with *cualiare*, rennet extracted from a young goat. While resting, the curd thickens and solidifies to a point where it can be cut with a knife. The whey is drained and the curd is cut into thin slices into a wooden tub, its outer rings tarnished with use and age. Mario adds boiling water to the curd and stirs with a narrow wooden paddle until the bulk is one solid mass again. He stretches and pulls and kneads the mass until it is smooth and pliable. Then Mario and Francesco sit down together to work it by hand. The mass is divided, and they continue to knead by hand in the scalding water, working out the air and water and shaping the ultimate form. The two men work silently with the rhythm of familiarity. Sitting on a *piesciolo*, a three-legged wooden stool made from forked tree branches, they knead and stretch the cheese with a meditative cadence. Caciocavallo is made only in June. In one day they will make three or four cheeses, depending on the amount of milk they collect. The last step is one more dip in boiling water to seal it, then it is cooled in the fresh spring water. The cheeses spend a few days in salted water, after which they are hung to age in the cool, dark cellars of their home. Some of the forms go to pay their rent for the municipal land where the cows graze, but most are for the family's consumption.

*Cutting the curd.*

It is cool and calm here, compared to the heat and chaos of the lowlands. Conversation meanders, echoing the lazy flies making dull circles around us. Listening in on a dialogue laced with dialect, I pick up bits and pieces about Maria and Francesco's brother, Felice d'Elia, now on his way by foot from Altamura with his cows, a week's journey. Our lunch is simply cheese and Maria's freshly baked bread, along with a taste of some of the local mushrooms that she has preserved in wine vinegar. Time has stopped for me.

*Rent on the mountain land is paid in cheese.*

# CACIOCAVALLO IN FOGLIE DI LIMONE ALLA GRIGLIA

*Caciocavallo Grilled in Lemon Leaves* - Cecilia Baratta Bellelli

The fragrant lemon leaves of southern Italy scent this Cilento coastal dish. It can be served as an antipasto or as a main course.

*1 pound caciocavallo cheese,
    sliced ¼ inch thick*

*12 large fresh lemon leaves*

*Extra-virgin olive oil for brushing*

❧ Prepare a fire in a grill.

❧ Trim the caciocavallo slices so that they are slightly smaller than the lemon leaves. Place a slice between 2 leaves like a sandwich. Close the edges with toothpicks. Brush the lemon leaves lightly with olive oil.

❧ Place the bundles on the grill and grill, turning once, until the cheese is slightly melted, 2 to 3 minutes on each side. Serve hot, reserving the leaves for garnish.

*SERVES 6*

# TIMBALLO DI MACCHERONI

*Pasta Timbale* - Cecilia Baratta Bellelli

Azienda Agrituristica Seliano is the estate of Cecilia Baratta Bellelli, located near the Magna Grecian ruins of Paestum. The Bellelli family has owned this property since 1830. Today the nineteenth-century guest house is a welcome stop for visitors, especially when Cecilia is in the kitchen. This elaborate timbale is a main dish usually served only on festive occasions. It can be made ahead and served at room temperature.

℘ To make the sauce, drain the mushrooms, reserving the liquid. Chop the mushrooms coarsely and set aside. Strain the liquid through a sieve lined with cheesecloth and set aside separately.

℘ In a large skillet over medium-high heat, warm the olive oil. Add the prosciutto and sauté until softened, but not browned, 2 to 3 minutes. Add the garlic, onion, carrot, and celery and sauté until golden brown, 3 to 4 minutes longer. Add the mushrooms and the ground meat to the pan and cook, stirring, until the mixture is golden brown, 5 to 7 minutes. Add the mushroom soaking liquid and the tomato paste, stir well, reduce the heat to low, cover, and cook until slightly thickened, about 1½ hours. Season with salt and pepper. Remove from the heat. Strain the sauce, reserving both the solids and the liquid. Set aside separately.

℘ To make the meatballs, in a bowl, combine the ground meat, egg, Parmigiano-Reggiano cheese, parsley, and milk-soaked bread. Season with salt and pepper. Shape into balls ¾ inch in diameter. Roll lightly in flour and set aside on a platter until ready to cook.

℘ In a skillet, pour in olive oil to a depth of ½ inch. Place over medium-high heat until hot but not smoking. Add the meatballs and cook, turning frequently, until browned on all sides, 8 to 10 minutes. Using a slotted spoon, remove to paper towels to drain.

℘ To make the pastry, in a large bowl, stir together the flour, sugar, and salt. With a pastry blender, cut the butter into the flour mixture until it is the consistency of coarse meal. Stir in the egg and just enough milk to bring the dough together. Divide the dough into 2 portions, one twice as large as the other. Flatten each portion into a disk and wrap separately in plastic wrap. Refrigerate for 1 hour or as long as 8 hours.

℘ While the dough is chilling, prepare the pasta. Bring a large saucepan of water to a boil. Add the pasta and cook for 8 minutes, or about 2 minutes less than if you were cooking until al dente. Drain and place in a bowl with the liquid from the sauce. Add the Parmigiano-

**For the sauce:**

2 ounces dried porcini, soaked in 1 cup warm water to soften for 20 minutes

1 cup extra-virgin olive oil

7 ounces prosciutto, finely chopped

1 clove garlic, minced

1 onion, diced

1 carrot, peeled and diced

1 celery stalk, diced

1 pound ground veal and/or pork

3 tablespoons tomato paste

Salt and freshly ground pepper to taste

**For the meatballs:**

½ pound ground veal and/or pork

1 egg

¼ cup grated Parmigiano-Reggiano cheese

2 tablespoons minced fresh flat-leaf parsley

2 slices day-old country-style bread, soaked in 1 cup milk

Salt and freshly ground pepper to taste

Unbleached all-purpose flour for dredging

Olive oil for frying

## For the pastry:

2⅜ cups (10½ ounces) unbleached
    all-purpose flour

2 teaspoons sugar

2 teaspoons salt

7 tablespoons chilled unsalted butter

1 egg, lightly beaten

About 3 tablespoons milk

## For the pasta:

1 pound zitone or penne

½ cup grated Parmigiano-Reggiano cheese

2 eggs, lightly beaten

## For assembly:

1 pound caciocavallo cheese,
    sliced ¼ inch thick

4 hard-boiled eggs, peeled and sliced
    ¼ inch thick

1 egg, lightly beaten, for egg wash

Reggiano cheese, stir to mix, and set aside to cool. When cool, stir in the eggs.

    🙟 To assemble, preheat an oven to 350°F.

    🙟 On a floured work surface, roll out the larger ball of dough into a round ⅛ inch thick. Transfer the round to a 12-inch springform pan, pressing the dough gently into the bottom and sides. Trim the edges, leaving a ¼-inch overhang.

    🙟 Spoon the reserved meat-vegetable solids from the sauce into the dough-lined pan. On top of the meat, layer one-fourth each of the caciocavallo, the hard-boiled egg slices, the meatballs, and then the pasta. Repeat the layers three more times to fill the pan.

    🙟 Roll out the remaining dough ⅛ inch thick and use to cover the *timballo*, pinching the edges together with the overhang of the bottom crust to seal. Brush the top with the egg wash. Chill for at least 30 minutes or as long as 2 hours.

    🙟 Bake until golden brown, about 45 minutes. Remove to a wire rack to cool for 10 minutes, then release the ring and slide the *timballo* onto a serving platter. Serve at once, warm, or at room temperature, cut into wedges.

SERVES 10

# MELANZANE SPACCATELLE

*Baked Eggplant* - Cecilia Baratta Bellelli

In southern Italy, eggplant is a staple. The name of this dish translates literally as "cracked eggplant," possibly alluding to the terrain around Pompei. It is a hearty vegetable dish that makes a fine main course. You can substitute provolone cheese if caciocavallo is not available.

✒ Preheat an oven to 325°F. Lightly oil a flameproof 9-by-13-inch baking pan.

✒ Cut each eggplant in half vertically. Make several crosshatches on the cut surface of each half to ensure even cooking. Place the halves in salted cold water to cover (about 3 tablespoons salt for each 8 cups water) for 10 minutes. Remove, rinse, pat dry, and place in the prepared baking pan, cut sides up. They should fit snugly.

✒ In a bowl, combine the tomatoes, olive oil, garlic, and basil. Mix well, season with salt, and mix again. Taste and adjust the seasoning. Spread the tomato mixture evenly over the eggplants and cover the pan. Bake until the eggplant is tender when pierced with a fork and the sauce has thickened, 50 to 60 minutes. Remove from the oven.

✒ Turn the oven to broil. Arrange the cheese slices evenly over the tops of the eggplant halves. Slip the pan under the broiler until the cheese melts and is golden brown, about 5 minutes. Serve at once.

*SERVES 4*

*2 large eggplants, about 1½ pounds total weight*

*1 pound ripe tomatoes, peeled and coarsely chopped*

*2 tablespoons extra-virgin olive oil*

*2 cloves garlic, minced*

*2 tablespoons minced fresh basil*

*Salt to taste*

*3 ounces caciocavallo cheese, sliced ¼ inch thick*

# CACIOCAVALLO ALLA PIZZAIOLA

*Pizza Maker's Cheese* - Cecilia Baratta Bellelli

This dish is named for its resemblance to the topping on a baked pizza. The flavor of the cheese, introduced by means of a smoky straw fire, is similar to that produced by a wood-burning pizza oven. This mixture is delicious as a spread on bread or spooned over roasted vegetables. Dried Greek marjoram is a good substitute for the wild marjoram; reduce the amount to ½ teaspoon.

¼ cup extra-virgin olive oil

1½ cups peeled and coarsely chopped
    ripe tomatoes, or 1 can (12 ounces) plum
    tomatoes, coarsely chopped, with juice

1 clove garlic, minced

10 ounces smoked caciocavallo cheese, grated

Salt to taste

1½ teaspoons minced fresh wild marjoram

6 to 8 fresh basil leaves

In a large skillet over medium heat, warm the olive oil. Add the tomatoes and garlic and cook, stirring occasionally, until the tomatoes have softened and released their juices, 10 to 15 minutes. Reduce the heat to low and cook for 5 minutes. Add the smoked cheese and stir until melted. Season to taste with salt, add the marjoram, and transfer to serving dish. Garnish with fresh basil leaves and serve at once.

*SERVES 4*

# MOZZARELLA DI BUFALA
## Cecilia Baratta Bellelli, *buffalo milk producer*
## Casearia Barlotti, *cheese cooperative*
### Paestum (Campania)

*It is hot here. It's not even officially summer yet, but the air is heavy with humidity from the surrounding water—water from the sea, and from the fields where the water buffalo are grazing. For a moment I imagine I hear the* cantilena, *the song used to call the buffalo for milking.*

*Seliano, June 1998*

The province of Salerno, south of Naples, is reputed to produce some of Italy's best fresh mozzarella made from the milk of the water buffalo. Exactly how the water buffalo came to be in Italy is unknown. It may be a native of the Mediterranean, or the first animals may have arrived from Asia in the eleventh century. It was initially valued primarily for use as a work animal because its hooves allowed it to tread the soggy plains. Today it is a prized dairy animal with a value of several thousand dollars per head.

Cecilia Baratta Bellelli and her sons, Ettore and Ernesto Massimino, carry on the tradition of their forebears, who have raised water buffalo here since the 1800s. Their estate, Azienda Agrituristica Seliano, located near the ruins of Paestum, covers ninety hectares (over two hundred acres) on the plains near the Tyrrhenian Sea. The land was a swamp until the 1930s, when Mussolini created the *Consorzio Bonifica* to drain and farm the region. Today Cecilia is on the board of directors for the present form of the *consorzio,* the water control district for the left bank of the Sele River. She helps decide how water will be distributed for irrigation and for the survival of the water buffalo.

*Mozzarella di bufala* is a fresh cheese produced entirely from full-fat buffalo milk. It was not developed

*Baroness Cecilia Baratta Bellelli.*

to preserve milk as most cheeses were. It was and is made to feature the fresh flavors of the milk, and is best consumed within forty-eight hours. There is a mozzarella made from cow's milk as well, called *fior di latte*. It is a less expensive product, not only because it is made in greater volume, but also because of the difference in the milk and in the cheese itself. The milk of the water buffalo has three times the fat of cow's milk. In addition, it is 1½ percent higher in calcium and protein.

Milk from Cecilia's herd of 550 buffalo is brought daily to the Casearia Barlotti, a cheese-making cooperative where all the work is done by hand. In the early morning, as soon as the fresh milk is delivered, it is heated to just a little over 100°F. This is the only time the milk will be heated; it is not pasteurized in this artisanal product. Industrial producers, especially if they plan to export it, do pasteurize the milk. "Pasteurizing kills the flavor," says Ettore. "You can't compare handmade *mozzarella di bufala* with the industrial product. They put the milk in a machine and instantly have mozzarella. We prefer it made by hand."

A natural rennet is added to the heated milk for coagulation. Once the curds have developed, they

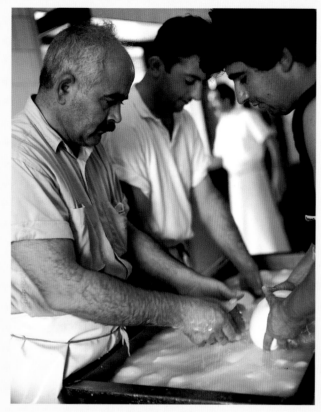

*Kneading the curd.*

mouthfuls," weighing less than two ounces. Larger rounds can range from a quarter of a pound to a pound and a half. The most beautiful of the lot are the braids, which are called *trecce*.

The name *mozzarella* comes from the action of breaking off—*mozzare*—the cheese with the hands. This is the mark of an artisanal mozzarella. The industrial product, mass-produced, is perfectly round and smooth. In a handmade cheese, you can see the lines left from when the cheese was torn off.

There is nothing like a bite of the still-warm cheese, oozing with milk. Cecilia says the best use of *mozzarella di bufala* is in the summer when it is too hot to go into the kitchen to cook. She serves it fresh at room temperature, complemented with vine-ripened tomatoes, fresh basil leaves, and estate-bottled olive oil. Who can argue with that?

*The milk of water buffalo has three times the fat of cow's milk.*

are broken into small pieces, the whey is drained away (but saved to make ricotta), and the curd is left to rest for two to four hours, depending on the temperature of the room and the quality of the milk. The cheese maker tests to see if it is ready by dropping a piece in boiling water. He squeezes it gently to see if it retains its shape. If it does, the curd is transferred to wooden vats of boiling water and kneaded with a wooden stick.

The cheese makers work in pairs: one man picks up a mass while another tears off small pieces to shape, working the hot mass into individual forms and leaving them to cool in brine. The finished cheese is porcelain white and slightly elastic from the kneading process. After a few hours it relaxes and becomes creamier.

There are several different forms and sizes. The smallest are called *cardinalini* or *bocconcini*, "little

# INSALATA CAPRESE

*Tomato and Mozzarella Salad from Capri* - Cecilia Baratta Bellelli

Fresh mozzarella is especially divine when partnered with Cecilia's estate-grown olive oil and pungent basil. The cherry tomatoes she uses are grown in the rich and dry soil of Mount Vesuvio. Called *spongili pomodorini*, they are often harvested still on their stalks and hung like bunches of grapes to use over the winter. If using large tomatoes and balls of mozzarella, slice them and arrange them on a platter, as shown in the photo below.

*6 small balls* mozzarella di bufala *cheese*
    (bocconcini or cardinalini),
    *about 2 ounces each*

*1 pint cherry tomatoes*

*½ cup extra-virgin olive oil*

*Salt to taste*

*12 large fresh basil leaves*

&#9758; Thread each cheese ball onto a 6-inch skewer along with the tomatoes, evenly dividing the tomatoes among the skewers. Arrange on a platter and drizzle with the olive oil. Season with salt and scatter the basil leaves on top. Serve at room temperature.

*SERVES 6*

# MOZZARELLA IN CARROZZA
*Deep-fried Mozzarella Sandwich*

Hot and creamy, "mozzarella in a carriage" is an excellent side dish to serve with soup or as a light lunch with a green salad. For another version, use arugula and prosciutto in place of the basil and tomato.

❧ Place 4 bread slices on a work surface. Arrange slices of mozzarella on each bread slice to cover, but not overlap, the edges. Top each with a basil leaf and a tomato slice. Season with salt and pepper and cover with the remaining 4 bread slices to form sandwiches.

❧ Dip the edges of each sandwich in the milk and pinch to seal. Dredge the sandwiches in the flour and then place them in a shallow dish.

❧ In a small bowl, lightly beat the eggs. Season with salt and pepper and pour over the sandwiches. Let stand for 10 minutes, lifting the sandwiches with a spatula to be sure the egg soaks all sides.

❧ In a skillet, pour in olive oil to a depth of 1 inch. Place over medium heat until hot but not smoking. Add the sandwiches and fry, turning once, until golden brown, 3 to 4 minutes on each side.

❧ Using a slotted spatula, remove to paper towels to drain briefly. Arrange on a platter and serve at once.

*SERVES 4*

*8 slices country-style bread, each ½ inch thick, crusts trimmed*

*½ pound mozzarella di bufala cheese, sliced ½ inch thick*

*8 basil leaves*

*1 tomato, cut into 8 thin slices*

*Salt and freshly ground pepper to taste*

*1 cup milk*

*1 cup unbleached all-purpose flour*

*2 eggs*

*Olive oil for frying*

# PIZZA RUSTICA
*Pizza with Mozzarella and Ricotta* ~ Cecilia Baratta Bellelli

Cecilia serves this hearty *torta* for informal get-togethers or as a main dish for a casual luncheon. If you are unable to find fresh buffalo ricotta, you can substitute a cow's milk version. Fresh buffalo mozzarella is preferred, but any soft cheese can be used.

*2 cups unbleached all-purpose flour*

*¾ teaspoon sugar*

*¾ teaspoon salt, plus salt to taste*

*2 eggs*

*5 tablespoons dry white wine*

*5 tablespoons extra-virgin olive oil*

*14 ounces (scant 2 cups)* ricotta di bufala *cheese*

*7 ounces* mozzarella di bufala *cheese, coarsely chopped*

*¼ pound* salame, *diced*

*Freshly ground pepper to taste*

❦ Preheat an oven to 375°F.

❦ In a large bowl, stir together the flour, sugar, and ¾ teaspoon salt. Stir in 1 egg, the wine, and the olive oil until blended. Transfer to a floured work surface and knead until smooth, about 5 minutes. Set aside to rest for 15 minutes.

❦ In a medium bowl, combine the ricotta, mozzarella, *salame*, and the remaining egg. Mix together until evenly blended. Season with salt and pepper. Set aside.

❦ Divide the dough in half. On a floured work surface, roll out half of the dough into a round ¼ inch thick. Transfer the round to a 10-inch pie pan, pressing the dough gently into the bottom and sides. Trim the edges even with the pan rim. Transfer the ricotta mixture to the dough-lined pan; smooth the surface.

❦ Roll out the remaining dough ¼ inch thick and cut into strips ½ inch wide. Place half of the strips across the filled pie pan, about ½ inch apart. Set aside enough strips to cover the rim of the pan, and arrange the remaining strips perpendicular to the first strips, weaving them with the first strips to create a lattice crust. Place the reserved strips around the rim of the pan to cover the ends of the strips and create an attractive edge.

❦ Bake until golden brown, about 45 minutes. Serve at once.

*SERVES 6*

# TYPICAL REGIONAL CHEESES

The majority of the milk produced in Italy is from cows and buffalo, with the remainder from sheep and goats. Over half of the milk produced goes into making more than four hundred different cheeses. A number of these unique regional products are protected by the DOC designation (denominazione di origine controllata), *a system that identifies the process by which a cheese is made and designates the specific zone in which it can be produced.*

*The world of Italian cheese is a complex one. Textures run the gamut from fresh and creamy to semihard and hard. There are stretched, soft, and blended cheeses; some made with animal rennet, others from vegetable sources; and shapes that vary from round, square, cylindrical, and hexagonal to pear-shaped and braided. Balls of cheese may weigh as little as a few ounces up to seventy-five pounds or more.*

*Many factors contribute to the making of an excellent cheese: good milk from particular breeds of cows,* sheep, or goats; quality fodder and proper treatment of the animals; traditional methods of processing; and the fine touch of the maker.

*Vacche Rosse, the ancient breed of cow in Emilia-Romagna.*

*Giovanni Goria, minister of Agriculture and Forests, the arm of government responsible for the supervision of DOC cheeses, says that when performing inspections, "careful attention is paid to the general context to provide an effective safeguard and useful promotion of quality, as well as of the human contributions with due concern for the original characteristics of the area of production."*

*While some cheeses such as Parmigiano-Reggiano, Gorgonzola, and mozzarella have achieved international fame, there remain many extraordinary cheeses that will only be found in the region of their production. Some cheeses, such as grana padano, stretch over several regions. On the following page I have listed some of the typical cheeses that you should seek out when you visit Italy.*

## ABRUZZO/MOLISE

Caciocavallo – *Medium pear-shaped form from cow's milk, aged three months to two years*

Scamorza Molisana – *Stretched cow's milk, dried forty-eight to seventy-two hours, sometimes smoked*

## APULIA

Burrata delle Murge – *Small elongated form from stretched cow's milk cheese filled with mozzarella and whey, wrapped in local flowers*

Canestrato Pugliese – *Medium round from sheep's milk, ripened in baskets for two months to one year*

## BASILICATA

Provolone – *Variety of shapes and sizes from cow's milk, aged three to twelve months*

Casieddu di Moliterno – *Fresh round from goat's milk flavored with* nepitella, *wrapped in ferns*

Cacioricotta – *Aged ricotta*

## CALABRIA

Caciocavallo – *Medium pear-shaped form from cow's milk, aged three months to two years*

Ricotta Affumicata – *Smoked ricotta*

## CAMPANIA

Mozzarella di Bufala – *Fresh balls of various sizes from milk of water buffalo*

## EMILIA-ROMAGNA

Parmigiano-Reggiano – *Large round from cow's milk, aged eighteen months to three years*

## LAZIO

Pecorino Romano – *Large cylinder from sheep's milk, aged eight to twelve months*

Cacioricotta – *Fresh small rounds from milk of sheep and goats*

## LIGURIA

Caprino d'alpeggio – *Small round from goat's milk, aged in natural caves*

## LOMBARDY

Gorgonzola – *Large round from inoculated cow's milk*

Taleggio – *Medium round from cow's milk, aged one to two months*

## MARCHES

Casciotta – *Fresh mixed milk*

## PIEDMONT

Bra – *Large round from cow's milk, aged two to three months*

Castlemagno – *Medium cylinder from cow's milk, aged two to five months*

Raschera – *Large, flat square from mixed milk, aged one to two months*

Robiola di Roccaverano – *Small, soft round from milk of goats, and sheep, sold fresh or aged to twenty days*

## SARDINIA

Fiore Sardo – *Small round from sheep's milk, aged up to six months*

Pecorina Sardo – *Small round from sheep's milk, aged two months*

## SICILY

Pecorino Siciliano – *Medium cylinder from sheep's milk, aged three to eighteen months*

Piacintinu di Enna – *Small round from sheep's milk, with saffron and whole black peppercorns, aged three to six days*

## TOSCANA

Pecorino Toscano – *Large cylinder from sheep's milk, aged one to three months*

Marzolino di Chianti – *Small oval from sheep's milk, traditionally coagulated with wild artichoke*

## TRE VENEZIE

Asiago – *Large round from cow's milk, aged three to nine months*

Montasio – *Large cylinder from cow's milk, aged three to eighteen months*

## UMBRIA

Caciotta – *Fresh small round from mixed milk*

Formaggio di Fossa al Talamello – *Mixed milk aged in tufa for three-and-a-half months*

## VAL D'AOSTA

Fontina – *Large, flat round from cow's milk, aged three to eight months*

# PARMIGIANO-REGGIANO
## Luciano Catellani, *president of CVPARR*
## Nello Faroni, *cheese maker*
### Cavriago (Emilia-Romagna)

*Here in Parmigiano-Reggiano land, I expected to see pastoral scenes of cows grazing on the hillsides, but I haven't seen any! But I have seen many cheese-making shops along the via Emilia. We stopped at one that had a sign in the form of a large three-dimensional cheese which carried the message "vendita diretta." The cheese maker gave us a mini tour of his mini factory. After showing us the large cheeses bobbing in salted water and aging on shelves in a cool room, he took down one of the giant wheels. He wedged a larger and larger crack down the center of it until it split right in half. The color was ocher dotted with minute specks of white. He chipped off a generous chunk for us to taste. It was heaven.*

*Villa Cella, June 1984*

Luciano Catellani has singled out a cow and leads her with a simple rope looped around her head. Her leaving does not go unnoticed. Suddenly the air is filled with a cacophony of moos, bellows, and moans from those left behind. They jealously strain to see where she is going, some of them even rearing on their hind legs. She seems almost smug as she accompanies Luciano on the short walk, her udder fairly bursting.

Only a few of the original Italian cattle breeds remain today. Of them, the Tuscan white Chianina is probably the most widely recognized. Most of Emilia-Romagna's cows were lost in World War II, and those remaining after the war were phased out due to their low milk yield compared to the newly arriving Dutch Holsteins. Over time, these newcomers were selected and improved by breeders, and the Frisona Italiana was born. They now number approximately two hundred thousand, and are the primary cow used by the

*Luciano Catellani.*

producers of Parmigiano-Reggiano. Their nickname is "milk machine," referring to the twenty-five-liter-per-day average each produces.

A few of the ancient breed, the Razza Reggiana, including Luciano's cow, survived. This tawny work animal, also know as *vacca rossa,* "red cow," was the historic provider of the milk for Parmigiano-Reggiano cheese, but her volume could not compare to that of the newer breeds. There is another difference, though, in her favor. The milk she produces is richer and higher in protein—in particular casein, the element that enables cheese to age longer.

In the sixties, there were only 75,000 head of Razza Reggiana in the whole region, a drop from the 1955 census of 130,000. Things got worse, and in less than a decade, by 1970, the number was down to 3,000. Dairy farmer Domenico Catellani was one of the last remaining breeders of the Reggiana. He and his two sons began the "rebellion" to bring back the

*Nello Faroni.*

breed as it swept to a dangerous low of 950 head in 1982. That was the year that Domenico's grandson Luciano returned from military service and went to work with his father and uncle. When Luciano was young, he remembers his father saying, "What is shining is not always gold," in reference to the full bucket of milk produced by the Frisona.

Today the count is back up to 2,000 head and growing. Luciano completed his studies at the university's *Istituto Tecnico Agrario A. Zanelli* in Reggio Emilia, an institute that has been doing research since 1972 on the coagulative properties of milk. In 1992, as part of his graduate studies, he brought his fifty cows to the university's experimental dairy, Notari. Over years of tracking, results have consistently shown that the milk of the Razza Reggiana is superior for cheese making. It has a different type of casein and other elements than the Frisona milk, characteristics that positively affect the time it takes for the milk to coagulate, the time it takes to harden, the consistency of the coagulation, the resistance to compression, and the resistance in cutting. The cream is richer, with better qualities. Even the butter-yellow color of the milk is considered exceptional.

In addition to the good news about the milk, studies found that medical costs were lower for this hearty breed, which had selected each generation to improve positive traits. Its members were stronger and had fewer illnesses. They ate less than the Frisona and lived three to four years longer. When all of these factors were taken into consideration, the breeders of Razza Reggiana realized that this was an economically viable animal, especially if the end product was a cheese that could undergo longer aging.

Since 1990, a group of ten Razza Reggiana breeders has been making cheese exclusively with Reggiana milk. The idea was born at a meeting of the two major breeders' associations. With 80 percent of its funding provided by the Ministry of Agriculture and Forest and the association with the university, a consortium was formed, the *Consorzio Valorizzazione Prodotti Antica Razza Reggiana* (CVPARR, the Consortium for the Improvement of Products of the Ancient Reggiana Race). The purpose of CVPARR is to improve the quality of the cheese made exclusively from Razza Reggiana milk. It supports this effort through study, experimentation, and application of new methods. Breeders are continually seeking to increase the number of head of cattle, and they support the development of artificial insemination.

Production is still small. In the zone where Parmigiano-Reggiano is made, three million wheels of cheese are produced annually. Only thirty-five hundred forms per year are from the Cooperative Notari, and half of them are made from the milk of the Razza Reggiana. Of these, four to five cheeses a day are made by Nello Faroni. Nello has been at Caseificio Notari for eleven years. Originally from Mantua, he started making cheese at the age of fifteen. With forty-three years of experience, he certainly knows what makes a good cheese, and he likes the milk of the red cow. "Cheese was born of the milk of the Razza Reggiana," he says.

Nello's day begins at the crack of dawn with the delivery of fresh milk. Stainless steel trays hold milk from the previous night's milking, which has been left to stand to allow the cream to separate and the milk to begin its fermentation. In the morning, part of the cream is removed and used for butter. The remaining partially skimmed milk is blended with the morning's whole milk and poured into huge bell-shaped copper vats to heat. Nello begins the cooking process by adding a portion of the whey from the previous day's cheese making, which has been fermenting overnight to develop the lactic flora needed to raise the acid content. He then introduces rennet to induce curdling.

As it cooks, the mixture begins to form soft curds and separates into solids and whey within fifteen minutes. Nello strains out pieces from time to time, testing them between his fingers to feel for the proper consistency. Then, when he determines the resistance is sufficient, he begins breaking the curd into tiny pieces with the *spino*, a large stainless steel tool that looks like a giant whisk. Once the curds are evenly riced, the mixture is heated again until it is precisely 55°C (131°F) and the curds have firmed; this takes twelve to fifteen minutes.

The mixture is left to rest and cool slightly for half an hour. Nello and his assistant capture the mass in a piece of cheesecloth, tie it to a large dowel, and hang it over the pot to drain. The cheese is then cut in half and kneaded into two separate rounds. Each half is placed in a circular plastic mold lined with cheesecloth and laid on a long wooden table. A heavy wooden disk is set on top to squeeze out some of the moisture and to keep the cheese from cooling too quickly. As it drains, it is turned and the cloth is changed every two hours. The cheese begins to firm up, and at the end of the day, the mold is temporarily removed to insert the Parmigiano-Reggiano stencil. This is a matrix of dots in a plastic band that will spell out the name Parmigiano-Reggiano in capital letters around the rim of the cheese. Also included in the impression is the month, year, and number of the dairy, in this case number 101. The mold is replaced and the cheese continues to drain for a few days, during which it is turned from top to bottom periodically to flatten both sides.

After two to three days of drying, the cheese will hold its shape. Nello removes the mold and brings the cheese to the brining and aging rooms. It remains in brine for twenty-two days and is turned daily to ensure that the salting is evenly distributed. After draining, the cheese is placed on wooden shelves to age for twelve months before it is inspected and approved by the *consorzio*. At this point most cheeses are kept in cheese

*The curd is drained from the whey.*

banks or with a distributor to age six months longer, for a total of eighteen months. This is where the Razza Reggiana pulls through: her cheese can age for up to three years. The amount of cream skimmed in the first step must be directly proportionate to the amount of casein in the milk. The ideal is to leave as much fat as possible in the milk, yet the protein content will only support so much. The greater the fat, however, the longer a cheese can age, and the more complex the final product.

The identifying brand on this cheese is a logo with two yoked red cows pulling a cart, harkening back to a time when cheese was transported without motor power. Luciano Catellani hopes to achieve sales of at least two thousand cheeses a year in the near future. This business will guarantee the realization of his grandfather's dreams.

# I LECCABAFFI
## Tagliolini *with Prosciutto and Parmigiano-Reggiano* ˜ Anna Cadoppi Piccirilli

Near Notari's cheese-making facility is the small, elegant Ristorante Picci. The chef, Anna Cadoppi, is an expert in regional foods such as prosciutto and Parmigiano-Reggiano. Marco, Anna's son, says the literal translation of this recipe is "The Dripping Moustache," so named for the way the delectable sauce is left in one's (or one's husband's) moustache when eating it!

℘ To make the pasta, mound the flour on a work surface. Make a well in the center, then crack the eggs into the well. Work the eggs into the dough with your fingertips, blending the flour a little at a time until fully incorporated. Knead until smooth, 10 to 15 minutes. Let rest for 15 minutes.

℘ With a rolling pin, roll out the dough into a very thin sheet. Hang the dough over the rolling pin to dry for about 15 minutes.

℘ Alternatively, use a hand-cranked pasta machine: start on the widest setting. Divide the dough into 3 or 4 portions. Keep all but the portion you are working with covered. Put each portion through the first setting 8 to 10 times, folding it in half each time, until the dough is smooth. If the dough tears, it may be too wet; dust it with flour, brushing off the excess. Continue putting the dough through the rollers without folding it, using a narrower setting each time, until it is the desired thickness. Leave the sheets on a floured cloth or hang them over the rolling pin to rest and dry for about 15 minutes.

℘ Meanwhile, make the sauce: In a small saucepan over low heat, melt the butter, then whisk in the flour. Cook, stirring, over low heat for 3 to 4 minutes to cook away the raw taste of the flour. Do not allow to brown. Add the milk, stirring constantly, raise the heat to medium, and continue to cook, stirring occasionally, until thickened, 3 to 5 minutes. Set aside.

℘ Roll up the pasta sheet and cut crosswise into fine strips to make *tagliolini* as thin as angel hair. Set aside on a floured surface.

℘ Preheat a broiler. In a skillet over medium heat, warm the olive oil. Add the mushrooms and sauté until softened, 2 to 3 minutes. Stir in the parsley, remove from the heat, and keep warm.

℘ Bring a large saucepan of salted water to a boil. Add the pasta, stir well, and cook until al dente, about 2 minutes. Drain the pasta and place in a large bowl. Add the mushrooms, *prosciutto cotto*, and cream. Season with salt and pepper. Mix well and place in a flameproof 9-by-13-inch baking dish. Cover with the sauce and top with Parmigiano-Reggiano cheese. Place under the broiler until lightly browned, 5 to 6 minutes. Serve at once.

*For the pasta:*

3¼ cups unbleached all-purpose flour

4 eggs

*For the sauce:*

2 tablespoons unsalted butter

2 tablespoons unbleached all-purpose flour

1 cup milk

3 tablespoons extra-virgin olive oil

3½ ounces fresh portobello mushrooms, thinly sliced

1 tablespoon minced fresh flat-leaf parsley

3½ ounces cooked prosciutto cotto (cooked ham), cut into strips

½ cup heavy cream

Salt and freshly ground pepper to taste

½ cup grated Parmigiano-Reggiano cheese

*SERVES 6*

# CAPRICCIO DI FUNGHI AL PARMIGIANO-REGGIANO

*Mushroom Whimsy with Parmigiano-Reggiano* - Anna Cadoppi Piccirilli

Some walls in the Ristorante Picci have fashion illustrations done by owner Quirino Piccirilli, leftovers from his first career. His second career is that of restaurant owner, and it has been a fine one indeed for the last nineteen years. The family also makes its own *aceto balsamico tradizionale*, which is served and sold in the restaurant.

To make the pastry, in a bowl, stir together the flour, sugar, and salt. Mix well. Add the butter, working it into the flour mixture with your fingertips until the mixture is the consistency of coarse meal. Add the water, a tablespoon at a time, working it into the dough until it comes together in a soft ball. Knead gently until smooth. Wrap in plastic wrap and refrigerate for at least 1 hour or as long as 8 hours.

Preheat an oven to 350°F. Butter four 8-ounce ramekins.

Using half of the Parmigiano-Reggiano slices, cover the bottoms of the baking dishes. Top each layer of cheese with one-fourth of the mushrooms, followed by a layer of one-fourth of the potato slices. Sprinkle the parsley evenly over the tops, then arrange a final layer of the remaining Parmigiano-Reggiano slices.

Divide the dough into 4 equal portions. On a floured work surface, roll each portion ⅛ inch thick into a shape suitable for covering the ramekins. Transfer to the tops of the ramekins, trimming off the excess dough and pressing the edges firmly around the rims to seal. Brush the pastry with the egg yolk and pierce with the tines of a fork.

Bake until lightly browned, 20 to 25 minutes. Remove from the oven and serve at once.

*SERVES 4*

## For the pastry:

2 cups unbleached all-purpose flour

2 teaspoons sugar

Pinch of salt

½ cup (4 ounces) chilled unsalted butter, cut into 8 equal pieces

3 tablespoons cold water

½ pound Parmigiano-Reggiano cheese, sliced ⅛ inch thick

½ pound fresh porcini or portobello mushrooms, sliced ¼ inch thick

2 potatoes, peeled, boiled until tender, and sliced crosswise ¼ inch thick

1 tablespoon minced fresh flat-leaf parsley

1 egg yolk, lightly beaten

# BUDINO DI PERE E PARMIGIANO-REGGIANO

*Pear Pudding and Parmigiano-Reggiano* - Anna Cadoppi Piccirilli

There is an Italian proverb that warns never to let the peasant taste how delicious pears and cheese are together. At Ristorante Picci, Anna Cadoppi serves this example of just how well the two flavors marry.

**For the poached pear garnish:**

*3 cups full-bodied red wine*

*⅔ cup sugar*

*2 tablespoons fresh orange juice*

*1 teaspoon grated orange zest*

*3 firm pears, peeled, halved, and cored*

**For the pudding:**

*4 cups milk*

*½ cup grated Parmigiano-Reggiano cheese*

*2 cups sugar*

*3 tablespoons water*

*7 egg yolks*

*1 egg white*

*2 firm pears, peeled, cored, and pureed in a food processor*

*Pinch of salt*

To make the poached pear garnish, in a saucepan over medium-high heat, combine the wine, sugar, orange juice, and orange zest and bring to a boil, stirring constantly. Reduce the heat to medium-low and simmer, stirring constantly, until the sugar dissolves. Add the pears, weighting them so that they are submerged in the liquid. Cover and cook just until the pears are tender, 30 to 40 minutes. Do not overcook. With a slotted spoon, remove the pears to a plate to cool. Discard the liquid.

To prepare the pudding, lightly butter eight 6-ounce ramekins.

Pour the milk into a saucepan and bring to a boil over medium heat. Add the Parmigiano-Reggiano, remove from the heat, and let cool.

While the milk is cooling, place 1 cup of the sugar and the water in a heavy-bottomed saucepan over low heat. Stir gently until the sugar is dissolved. Continue cooking, without stirring, until the mixture is a rich, deep caramel color, about 5 minutes. Remove from the heat and pour into the prepared ramekins, dividing evenly. Set aside.

Preheat an oven to 275°F.

In a bowl, combine the egg yolks and egg white. Whisk in the remaining 1 cup sugar, the pear pulp, and the salt. Add the cooled milk mixture, stir well, and pour into the ramekins, dividing evenly. Cover each ramekin with a piece of buttered parchment paper, buttered side down.

Bake until a toothpick inserted in the center of a pudding comes out clean, about 45 minutes. Let cool for 10 minutes, then invert onto individual plates. Garnish each pudding with half a poached pear and serve at once.

*SERVES 8*

# IV

# *FROM THE EARTH*

## WHITE TRUFFLES
Nereo Fenocchio

*No fresh truffles?*

## CAPERS
Antonino Caravaglio

## DRIED HERBS
Duccio Fontani

## COOKING FROM THE LAND
Carlo Cioni, *Da Delfina*

IV

*White truffles thrive in the rolling hills of Piedmont.*

# FROM THE EARTH

This chapter includes some of Italy's most treasured cooking ingredients—capers, truffles, herbs, and wild plants—and the passion its natives have for them. If you're lucky, you will arrive in a small village on the day of a festival, or sagra. Most communities have at least one celebration a year, usually more. It could be the day of the town's patron saint, a religious holiday, or a centuries-old celebration in honor of a local food product.

An hour's boat ride from Sicily, the tiny island of Salina holds its annual Sagra del Cappero on the first weekend of June. For two days, everyone turns out for a party atmosphere that culminates in visits to various producers and a final degustazione dei piatti tipici a base di capperi, "tasting of typical caper dishes." This closing event proved to be the best potluck dinner I've ever attended. Held in front of the church in the town of Pollara (where the movie Il Postino was filmed), the meal was laid out on a dozen long tables lined up end to end. Standing alongside the assortment of dishes were bottles of the local Malvasia wine. Children, elders, and young lovers mixed together and enjoyed the warm night. Massive pots of pasta were cooked somewhere inside the church, brought out, and tossed with a piquant salsa verde.

At the other end of the country is a source of another of Italy's culinary jewels. Since 1903, Alba, a quiet town in Piedmont, has been host to an internationally renowned agricultural and industrial fair, a month-long celebration of one of its products, the white truffle. The custom of holding a competition and intellectual discussions began in 1949, and has continued to this day with great success. Every weekend boasts a gastronomic and cultural calendar, but the main attraction is the truffle market. Twenty to thirty truffle hunters display their wares for sale and competition. The aroma in the room is heady and indescribable!

Serious celebration of the land's foods is an Italian custom, and lacing through the ceremonial dishes are the flavors of essential herbs, fresh and dried. Dishes come alive with leaves of mint, sage, and rosemary; flowers from fennel and saffron; and the seeds and berries of mustard, coriander, and juniper. Many of these grow wild. There are even festivals specifically in tribute to oregano and rosemary, recalling times of economic hardship when "living off the land" was a reality that involved a search for locally available wild foods.

In each of the regions where these extraordinary ingredients are found, home cooks and chefs have created innumerable ways to incorporate them into the local dishes.

*Piedmont is home to some of Italy's most exceptional wines.*

# WHITE TRUFFLES
## Nereo Fenocchio
### Alba (Piedmont)

*It is the first time I've been in Italy late enough to experience truffle season. I ordered risotto, and as I watched the waiter shaving paper-thin slices on top, like earthy rose petals, I couldn't help but think how generous he was. It wasn't until the bill came that I realized I was charged by the weight I had consumed.*

*Albaretto Torre, October 1992*

With the distant backdrop of the snow-covered Alps, and the rolling hills of the Langhe (Alba and south) and Roero (north of Alba) afire with autumn color, one hardly imagines that beneath the surface of this beautiful land grows an extraordinarily delectable fungus. Yet every night from the middle of September to the end of January, scruffy little dogs silently lead their owners to the underground riches known as *tartufi bianchi,* or "white truffles."

For thirty years, Nereo Fenocchio has called himself a *trifolao,* or "truffle hunter." Tobi, the thirteen-year-old favorite of his four dogs, watches his owner's face intently. With a glance, Nereo sends the sleek, freckled dog in one direction, then the other, "*Torna indietro*" (Go back) or "*Passa su*" (Go up there). A whistle stops the dog in his tracks. Nereo works steadfastly, observant of his companion's every movement. Tobi sniffs, and sniffs again, staring persistently at the base of an indigenous poplar tree. When he begins to scratch at the ground, Nereo intercedes with a treat of cheese, and Tobi backs off to watch the excavation.

Nereo learned his trade from his father, who learned from his father before him. "It is a family gift," he says. "It is not something you can just take up on

*Nereo Fenocchio and Tobi.*

your own. You must learn from experts. It's not only the hunting and the discovery techniques and the careful digging. It's also about establishing a successful relationship with the dog you have trained, caring for and respecting the forest, and taking the chance of wasting some time."

In the past, truffle hunters used pigs to seek out the riches underground. The French still do, but most of the hunters here prefer dogs. They are easier to train, eager to please their owner, and are not as interested in actually eating the truffle once they find it. The training is intense. It takes three years to teach a dog the art of wanting to search for the truffle, then giving it up once it has been located. The lessons begin at the age of two months. While in training, the pups are fed a scant diet, and when they are hungry, they are encouraged to search for a buried treasure. In the beginning, it is cheese, usually Gorgonzola. The strong aroma leads them to find just the right spot. Later, the hidden prize is changed to truffle, and when the truffle is found, the dog is rewarded with a piece of meat or cheese. The truffle is buried deeper in each training session, until the dog is able to sniff out the prize from a depth of eight to twelve inches. "I've trained over a hundred dogs; only half have become good hunters," Nereo explains. "The perfect dog should never dig the truffle out; that is the task of the *trifolao*. He should smell the truffle, go look for his owner, and show him the spot. Only if the dog knows the truffle is deep down will he help the hunter dig, with one paw or two, depending on the depth. If it is near the surface, the dog will just touch the spot with its paw and stay put."

These talented dogs are not of any particular breed. In fact, they are a "pure mutt race" that is honored every summer in a nearby village at the aptly named Mongrel Dog Fair. Small to medium in size and strong, they are a mixed breed selected for intelligence, sensitivity, and excellent sensory aptitudes of smell, eyesight, and hearing. Competition for dogs among truffle hunters is intense. Imagine the value of an animal that can uncover a commodity priced locally at seven hundred to nine hundred dollars per pound. As an export, the prices quickly rise into four figures. Dogs must be protected against such potential dangers as poisoning and theft. Most of them are kept under close supervision to safeguard them from jealous competitors.

Nereo, dressed in warm flannels and wools, a sweater vest, and a cap, does his work at night carrying only a stick, a small light, and a *zampin* (dialect for *zappina*), a narrow handmade spade. He says he goes out at night because there are no distractions and the perfume of the truffle is more prominent, but more likely he wishes to protect his secret sources.

Tobi is animated, curious at what Nereo has extracted. The scent fills the air, pungent and compelling. "Sometimes it can take up to three hours to dig up a 10-gram truffle," explains Nereo. The knobby orb looks like a swollen walnut, a yellow-tinged earthy buff color with an uneven surface. It is nearly an inch in diameter. Nereo says he once found one that weighed 600 grams (21 ounces). The size can vary, but the average is 30 to 100 grams (1 to 3½ ounces).

In local dialect the white truffle is called *trifola d'Alba*. It is classified as a tuber (*Tuber magnatum* 'Pico') and lives in a symbiotic relationship on the roots of trees, usually oak, willow, hazelnut, and poplar. "The truffles from different trees are unlike each other," says Nereo. "Oak ones have yellowish stripes. An egg-shaped truffle from an oak may weigh 30 grams more than the same shape from a poplar.

"It takes a truffle three moons to mature. They can be found from the middle of September to the end of January, but the best ones are in November and December." He says there is also one called the *tartufo dei quaranta giorni,* the forty-day truffle, which takes only one moon and ten days to develop and is found beneath the humus. "The perfect white truffle is round and smooth, with a fine smell, from an oak tree. It is the king of truffles, even though it is the least beautiful. It should weigh from 60 to 110 grams [2 to 4 ounces]. Anything above that weight is quite exceptional."

The best catches occur in the Roero, Langhe, and Monferrato areas. In the hills where the trees grow, the soil is dense, often composed of clay-limestone and flint. There is an historic competition between neighboring Asti truffle hunters and those in Alba, and Nereo concedes that "the Asti truffle is better looking, with a smooth surface and rounder shape." This is because "the tufa soil in the Alba area [unlike its sandy counterpart in Asti], which nourishes the Nebbiolo grape for our Barolo wine, doesn't allow the truffle to grow round and polished," Nereo explains. He says the most important factor in determining a good year is the humidity of the soil, "cold and snow in the winter, warm and rainy at the right times." It is, in fact, the opposite of what will make for a good year of grapes, so the weather will never please everyone.

After Nereo harvests Tobi's find, he carefully fills the hole in again to allow the root to produce future truffles. The truffle's growth is spontaneous, but regrowth is somewhat predictable due to the spores left behind. Once harvested, if handled properly, the truffle will remain fresh and fragrant for a week.

In order to hunt, Nereo pays a little over one hundred dollars per year to have a *Patentino*, a license to hunt that applies to anything wild, from boar to birds to truffles. He also has a *Tesserino Sanitario*, a permit that allows him to make sales. Most of what he finds, however, is for his family and friends, although he does sell some, mostly through word of mouth.

Truffle supplies have diminished by half in the last ten years. "The main problems are pollution and the ozone layer," according to Nereo, "which make the weather very irregular." Scatterings of white truffles are found in other parts of Italy. In years when weather has been poor and demand has surpassed supply, some *tartufi bianchi* from nearby regions have found their way here. The strongest competition comes from Acqualagna in the Marches, whose truffles are difficult to distinguish when they have been cleaned up and added to the market offerings. Small reserves also exist in Tuscany's Senese and in parts of Lazio, Emilia-Romagna, and Umbria.

The famous black truffle of the Périgord region in France can also be found in great numbers in central Umbria. The main variety is the *Tuber melanosporum* 'Vittadini.' Priced at half of what the white truffle commands, it is very aromatic and renders itself well in cooking. Like the white truffle, it is irregularly shaped, but its color is very black, with a metallic, reflective quality. It is found from the end of November into spring.

The white truffle should never be cooked. It is brought to the table and sliced over a freshly prepared hot dish. Many products have been developed to conserve the aroma and flavor of the truffle, such as paste in a tube, vacuum packing, pieces blended in butter, in garlic, in oil, in pâtés or terrines. Nereo's favorite way to eat truffles? "Shaved over an egg or on *fonduta*."

*Alba hosts a truffle fair every October.*

# TAJARIN AL BURRO E TARTUFO

*Pasta with Butter and Truffles* - Paolo Affori

For the last ten years, Paolo Affori has been the chef at some of the best restaurants around Alba. His menus feature regional specialties such as *tajarin* (dialect for *tagliolini*), a classic Piemontese pasta and the perfect foil for the white truffle. For a softer, more tender dough, Paolo recommends using only the egg yolks and adds 1 tablespoon olive oil to the pasta dough.

*For the pasta:*

*2¼ cups unbleached all-purpose flour, sifted*

*3 eggs*

*3 tablespoons unsalted butter*

*2 fresh sage leaves*

*¼ cup grated Parmigiano-Reggiano cheese*

Tartufo bianco d'Alba

@ To make the pasta, mound the flour on a work surface. Make a well in the center, then crack the eggs into the well. Gradually work the eggs into the dough with your fingertips, incorporating the flour a little at a time. When it is fully incorporated, knead until smooth, 10 to 15 minutes. Let rest for 15 minutes.

@ With a rolling pin, roll out the dough into a very thin sheet. Leave the sheet on a floured cloth or hang it over the rolling pin to rest and dry for about 15 minutes.

@ Alternatively, use a hand-cranked pasta machine to roll out the dough: Start on the widest setting. Divide the dough into 2 or 3 portions. Keep all but the portion you are working with covered with an overturned bowl. Put each portion through the first setting 8 to 10 times, folding it in half each time, until the dough is smooth. If the dough tears, it may be too wet; dust it with flour, brushing off the excess. Continue putting the dough through the rollers without folding it, using a narrower setting each time, until it is the desired thickness. Leave the sheets on a floured cloth or hang them over the rolling pin to rest and dry for about 15 minutes.

@ Roll up the pasta sheet(s) and cut crosswise into noodles as thin as possible. Set aside on a lightly floured surface.

@ In a small saucepan over medium heat, melt the butter until foaming. Add the leaves of sage and remove from the heat. Keep warm.

@ Bring a large saucepan of salted water to a boil. Add the pasta, stir well, and cook until al dente, about 2 minutes. Drain the pasta and transfer to a large serving bowl.

@ Add the sage-infused butter and toss well. Stir in the Parmigiano-Reggiano cheese. Using a truffle slicer or mandoline, shave thin slices of the white truffle over the pasta to cover. Serve at once.

*SERVES 4*

# UOVA TARTUFATO

*Truffled Egg in Pasta* - Paolo Affori

One of the most divine ways to consume truffles is to shave them on top of an over-easy egg. This dish perfectly marries a love for pasta and the egg-truffle combination. In Paolo's original version, the pasta was shaped like a ring, filled with the spinach-ricotta mixture, and cooked. Just before serving, he cracks a fresh raw egg in the center and tops it with truffle. I've created a variation that allows the egg to cook a little: it is hidden inside the pasta package and serves as a sauce when your fork pierces it.

**For the filling:**

*1 pound spinach, steamed and squeezed dry*

*7 ounces (scant 1 cup) ricotta cheese*

*½ cup grated Parmigiano-Reggiano cheese*

*1 large egg*

*Freshly grated nutmeg to taste*

*Salt and freshly ground pepper to taste*

**For the pasta dough:**

*1¼ cups unbleached all-purpose flour*

*2 large eggs*

*8 small eggs*

*3 tablespoons unsalted butter, melted and kept warm*

*Grated Parmigiano-Reggiano cheese*

Tartufo bianco d'Alba

To make the filling, in a food processor, combine the cooked spinach, ricotta cheese, Parmigiano-Reggiano cheese, and 1 egg. Process until smooth. Season with nutmeg, salt, and pepper. Set aside.

To make the pasta, mound the flour on a work surface. Make a well in the center, then crack the 2 eggs into the well. Gradually work the eggs into the dough with your fingertips, incorporating the flour a little at a time. When it is fully incorporated, knead until smooth, 10 to 15 minutes. If the dough is too hard, soften it with a few drops of water. Let rest for 15 minutes.

Divide the dough in half. With a rolling pin, roll out each half into a thin sheet. They should be the same size. Place 1 sheet on a lightly floured work surface. Set the other sheet aside on a floured surface.

Divide the filling into 8 equal portions and place the mounds on the pasta sheet, spacing them an equal distance apart. Form a nest in the center of each mound. Crack 1 small egg and separate it, slipping the yolk into one small dish and the white into another. Take care not to break the yolk. Slide the yolk into one of the nests. Repeat with the remaining small eggs, dropping a yolk into each nest and reserving the whites for another use.

Carefully lay the second sheet of pasta on top of the first. Press very gently around the mounds. Using a pasta wheel, cut around each nest. Pinch the edges to seal well. As each filled pasta is cut, place on a lightly floured surface.

Bring a large saucepan of salted water to a boil. Carefully slide the pasta packages into the boiling water and boil gently until al dente, about 2 minutes. Remove with a slotted spoon, draining well, and place directly onto warmed individual plates.

Dress the pasta with the melted butter and Parmigiano-Reggiano cheese. Using a truffle slicer or mandoline, shave thin slices of white truffle over the top of each serving. Serve at once.

*SERVES 4*

# FONDUTA AL TARTUFO

*Truffled Fontina Sauce* - Paolo Affori

Paolo's wife, Alessandra, and her family run Truffle Tours out of Alba (see Resources, page 163, for further information). After a chilly foray searching for truffles, Alessandra recommends a warming antipasto of *fonduta*, delicious for dipping lightly toasted bread. It can also be used as a sauce for vegetables or pasta.

℘ In a large heatproof bowl, combine the cheese and milk and let stand for 1 hour.

℘ Place the bowl in a wide pan. Add water to reach halfway up the sides of the bowl and place the pan over low heat. Cook, stirring constantly, until the little pieces of cheese have melted; do not allow to boil. In a medium bowl, whisk the eggs. Slowly add the hot mixture to the beaten egg, stirring constantly, to warm it up gently without curdling.

℘ Return the mixture to the pan of water and continue to simmer, whisking constantly, until smooth and slightly thickened, about 5 minutes.

℘ Transfer the *fonduta* to a dish with a warmer. Using a truffle slicer or mandoline, shave thin slices of white truffle over the top. Place the toasted bread on individual plates. Serve at once.

*MAKES 1½ CUPS; SERVES 4 TO 6*

½ pound Val d'Aosta Fontina cheese, grated

1 cup milk

5 egg yolks

Tartufo bianco d'Alba

Country-style bread, sliced and lightly toasted

# CARNE CRUDA ALL'ALBESE

*Veal Tartare, Alba Style* ~ Paolo Affori

One of Paolo Affori's specialties is this classic dish of Alba, made with chopped fresh meats. Mince the veal with a knife, rather than grinding it, for a better consistency.

*1 pound lean veal loin, finely chopped*

*3 tablespoons extra-virgin olive oil*

*1 tablespoon fresh lemon juice*

*1 clove garlic, minced*

*Salt and freshly ground pepper to taste*

Tartufo bianco d'Alba

❧ Place the chopped veal in a large bowl. In another bowl, combine the olive oil, lemon juice, and garlic. Mix well and season with salt and pepper. Stir into the chopped veal. Mix well.

❧ Divide the mixture among 5 individual plates, spreading it into a thin layer on each one. Using a truffle slicer or mandoline, shave thin slices of white truffle over the top of each plate. Serve at once.

*SERVES 5*

# CAPERS
## Antonino Caravaglio
### Isola Salina (Sicily)

*I was sitting just outside the fortress today when a man walked up and began picking something from the scrubby bush growing horizontally from the cracks in the walls. It turned out to be capers. He told me he would take the flower buds home and soak them in salt water for a month, then keep them in vinegar.*

*Siena, June 1992*

Although you can find capers in most of central and southern Italy, this native Mediterranean bush seems to flourish in the presence of the sun and the sea of Sicily, in particular in the volcanic and rocky soil of the Aeolian Islands. The plant has an orchid-like flower of white and violet that secretes a sweet nectar. Children love to suck it from the blooms. But when possible, the unopened flowers are "nipped in the bud" to become the pungent caper.

To get to the tiny island of Salina, you take one of the ferries that connect the Aeolians to Sicily. You arrive at the port of Santa Marina, its pier just large enough to accommodate the boat. At the land's end of the dock, you intersect the only road on Salina, a byway that dips in and out of volcanic craters and formations as it encircles the island. A few steps farther inland is the stone walking street that winds through Santa Marina. In one breath, you are part of the island mentality. Perhaps it is the heat, or the stillness, but everything suddenly slows.

A five-minute drive out of Santa Marina brings you a quarter of the way around the island to Malfa and the family home of Antonino "Nino" Caravaglio. It's hard to imagine this stocky man picking the delicate buds of the caper plant, but in the hot summer

*Antonino Caravaglio.*

months, on the rocky hillside overlooking the Tyrrhenian Sea, Nino does the work of harvesting and preserving the capers that grow on his land. The rest of the year is spent marketing and promoting the product and also tending his numerous vineyards. "The best variety is the *Cappero nocielo*. Although *C. spinoso* produces more," Nino explains, "we prefer the quality of the *nocielo*."

In June the picking begins. Just as the flowers begin to bud, the hillsides are swarming with children, their parents, and their grandparents picking every available bud. Ultimately, the capers will be preserved in salt, brine, or vinegar, but most of the locals agree that salt is the ideal medium for preserving flavor and plumpness.

Obviously it is not possible to catch every flower before it blooms. A second product, *cucuncio,* is derived from the mature stamen. Once the petals have dropped, the stamen swells and forms a large berry. When cured, it has the same piquant and peppery flavor as the capers.

The buds are brought to the warehouse and placed in large tubs, where they are tossed with coarse sea salt. As the capers sit in the tub, they release some of their liquids, which create a brine that is drained off every few days. New sea salt is added and

*Caper bushes on the island of Salina.*

the process repeated for two months. "The salt makes it sweeter, brings out the essence of the caper," Nino says as he goes about the work of refreshing the salt.

By August, the curing is done. The capers will have dried enough to pack in jars with fresh sea salt, ready to use. Production quantities are low. One plant will yield approximately ten pounds of capers in a season. From all of Nino's plants, he will pack only four hundred pounds of capers a year.

*Salt-cured capers retain their plumpness and flavor.*

*Capers are left under salt for two months.*

# INVOLTINI DI PESCE SPADA
*Stuffed Swordfish Rolls*

On Salina, fish fillets are typically rolled up with a variety of ingredients, always spiced with the island capers. Serve the swordfish rolls on a bed of sautéed spinach and garnish with lemon and tomato wedges.

*1 pound swordfish fillets*

*½ cup fine dried bread crumbs*

*½ cup minced onion*

*¼ cup grated Parmigiano-Reggiano cheese*

*¼ cup salt-cured capers, rinsed*

*¼ cup coarsely chopped green olives*

*2 tablespoons extra-virgin olive oil*

*1 tablespoon tomato sauce*

*1 tablespoon minced fresh flat-leaf parsley*

*Salt and freshly ground pepper to taste*

*Extra-virgin olive oil for grilling*

@ Prepare a fire in a grill.

@ Cut the swordfish into ½-inch-thick slices. Place the fish fillets between 2 sheets of plastic wrap. Using a meat pounder, gently flatten to an even thickness of ¼ inch.

@ In a medium bowl, combine the bread crumbs, onion, Parmigiano-Reggiano cheese, capers, olives, olive oil, tomato sauce, parsley, salt, and pepper. Mix well. Spread the mixture evenly onto the swordfish slices. Roll up each slice lengthwise and secure with toothpicks or kitchen string.

@ Brush the rolls with olive oil. Place on the grill and turn to cook on all sides until the fish is firm to the touch, but not dry, 8 to 10 minutes.

@ Remove the toothpicks or string from each roll. Cut crosswise into slices 1 inch thick. Arrange on a platter or individual plates and serve at once.

*SERVES 4*

# SALSA ROSSA PICCANTE
*Spicy Red Sauce*

This versatile sauce is found in many dishes on Salina. It can be made ahead and refrigerated until ready to use. Try it over pasta, grilled vegetables, or baked seafood.

    &#x2615; In a bowl, combine all the ingredients. Mix until well blended.

*MAKES ABOUT 1 CUP; SERVES 4*

*½ cup salt-cured capers, rinsed*

*4 anchovy fillets, mashed*

*3 tablespoons minced fresh flat-leaf parsley*

*3 tablespoons extra-virgin olive oil*

*3 tablespoons tomato sauce*

*2 cloves garlic, minced*

*1 tablespoon fresh lemon juice*

*Salt and freshly ground pepper to taste*

# CAPONATA ALLA SICILIANA

*Sicilian Caponata*

Serve this vegetable relish as a condiment for grilled seafood or poultry, or as a simple topping for toasted country bread.

*1 eggplant, about 1 pound, peeled and cut into ½-inch cubes*

*Salt for eggplant, plus salt to taste*

*¼ cup extra-virgin olive oil*

*1 onion, diced*

*3 cloves garlic, minced*

*3 tablespoons salt-cured capers, rinsed*

*2 tablespoons pine nuts, lightly toasted*

*2 teaspoons sugar*

*3 tablespoons red wine vinegar*

*1 cup peeled and diced ripe tomato*

*Salt and freshly ground pepper to taste*

❦ Spread the eggplant on several layers of paper towels and sprinkle with salt. Let stand for 10 minutes. Rinse and pat dry with paper towels.

❦ In a large sauté pan over medium heat, warm the olive oil. Add the onion and garlic and sauté until golden, 3 to 4 minutes. Add the eggplant and cook until softened, 2 to 3 minutes longer. Add the capers, pine nuts, sugar, and wine vinegar. Cook over medium heat until the vinegar evaporates, 3 to 4 minutes. Add the tomato and heat through, about 2 minutes. Season with salt and pepper. Serve at room temperature.

*SERVES 8*

# INSALATA DI MARE EOLIANA
*Aeolian Seafood Salad with Olives and Capers*

Any combination of seafood is nice with this simple dressing of olive oil and lemon juice. Try including some steamed mussels or calamari.

☙ In a large sauté pan over medium heat, warm ¼ cup of the olive oil. Add the onion and sauté until softened, 2 to 3 minutes. Do not allow to brown. Add the fish, shrimp, and scallops and cook until the fish and scallops are firm and the shrimp are pink, 3 to 5 minutes. Add the wine, raise the heat to high, and cook until the wine is almost evaporated, 2 to 3 minutes longer. Using a slotted spoon, remove the seafood mixture to a plate and let cool.

☙ Place the cooled seafood in a large bowl. Add the parsley, garlic, olives, and capers. Toss well. Add the remaining ¼ cup olive oil and the lemon juice and toss again. Season with salt, chile flakes, and pepper.

☙ Serve at room temperature.

*SERVES 4*

½ cup extra-virgin olive oil

¼ cup minced onion

1 pound assorted fish fillets such as
   sea bass, swordfish, and halibut,
   cut into 1-inch chunks

½ pound shrimp, peeled and deveined

½ pound sea scallops

¼ cup dry white wine

1 tablespoon minced fresh flat-leaf parsley

2 cloves garlic, minced

¼ cup pitted Mediterranean-style oil-cured
   black olives

⅓ cup salt-cured capers, rinsed

Juice of 1 lemon

Salt, red chile flakes, and freshly ground
   pepper to taste

# PEPERONATA
## Sweet Peppers and Capers

The summer sweetness of peppers contrasts well with the piquant caper. This colorful dish is excellent served as a side dish for seafood or poultry. Nino advises that salt-cured capers should be always added last to any dish as a seasoning, and never cooked.

¼ cup extra-virgin olive oil

2 large sweet onions, sliced

2 yellow bell peppers, sliced

2 red bell peppers, sliced

3 ripe tomatoes, peeled and coarsely chopped

1 tablespoon red wine vinegar

¼ cup salt-cured capers, rinsed

 In a large saucepan over medium heat, warm the olive oil. Add the onions and sauté until golden brown, 6 to 8 minutes. Add the yellow and red peppers and the tomatoes. Cook until the liquid released by the vegetables has evaporated and peppers are soft, 4 to 5 minutes.

 Remove from the heat and add the vinegar and capers. Mix well and transfer to a serving dish. Serve at room temperature.

*SERVES 6*

# DRIED HERBS
## Duccio Fontani
Tregole (Tuscany)

*In sleepy Castellina in Chianti I bought some little jars of dried herbs from a gentleman with a flower-laden cart. Amazing fragrant blends of flowers, seeds, and leaves. I can't wait to cook with them.*

*Castellina in Chianti, May 1991*

Since 1984, Duccio Fontani has been cultivating a piece of land in the village of Tregole, halfway between Castellina in Chianti and Fonterutoli. The rolling hills of Chianti are the perfect host for his *piante aromatiche da cucina*, "aromatic plants for cooking." The land he farms has a wild look to it, completely natural, with a small dirt road winding up to a tiny ancient cemetery laced with wild vines and flowers. Duccio says, "The cemetery is a peaceful place, in harmony with my work." These six hectares (almost fifteen acres) of land were abandoned in the fifties when much of the population of Tregole left for the industry of the cities. When Duccio arrived some thirty years later, he found an abundance of spontaneous vegetation: poppy, mustard, *nepitella* (a wild mint), wild rose hips, thyme, and juniper berries. He began collecting and drying the wild plants for his own kitchen. "We keep jars of *aromi* on the table like salt," he says. "I like it best raw or just barely cooked. My favorite way to eat it is on bread with oil.

"One beautiful day I thought I could make a living selling some of these dried herbs. I took them to the market and sold them all, and I went again the next week. Little by little, it evolved into a regular business." It was quite natural for Duccio to enhance the profusion with compatible cultivated aromatic plants.

*Duccio Fontani.*

The diverse microclimate of the farm runs from humid to arid and rocky. About one-third has now been organized into circular plantings and terraces, with wide open spaces of wild growth in between. A small spring provides some water, but most of the moisture comes from natural rainfall. The fertility of the land is maintained by the practice of composting, covering the soil with the remains of herb plants, straw, and leaves. Chemicals are not used, and all of the work is done by hand.

Only fifteen people now live in Tregole, with Duccio's family numbering five. His German-born wife and their three sons reside in the old schoolhouse. "For me, it is poetry to be close to the land. My children work on the farm, and they are happy." Schoolchildren aged six to thirteen are happy, too, to come in groups to visit the farm. "I want them to experience the importance of leaving the land natural. It is important for work and for health." And the children love the donkeys.

Since 1996, Duccio has had the help of five little donkeys. They answer with noisy brays when he calls them. He refers to the male as the "little man" with his harem. Their work is useful because they eat the grass, cleaning the corners that are difficult to treat by hand. Hedges and natural barriers of twigs and branches confine the donkeys to specific areas when needed. Their manure helps fertilize the fields. But Duccio values them especially for their company. "During the good season they accompany me on the long walks through the fields, in the woods, and across the river that borders the farm."

Harvest usually begins in May and continues to the end of October. The herbs are allowed to dry slightly on the plant to reach the full potential of their vine-ripened flavor. They are processed immediately after picking, as storage may jeopardize the quality of the finished product. First the stems hang in cloth sacks to dry for three days in the garden shed, where it is hot but shady. When the leaves are completely dry, they are pulverized by hand in a mortar and then blended "by inspiration." Approximately an ounce of herbs is packed into each small jar. The blend is handwritten on the label and the jar is sealed and placed among its colorful counterparts on Duccio's cart. He festoons his rolling herb market with fresh herbs, flowers, and ribbons, and then off he goes.

You can find Duccio every day from noon to one o'clock in the center of Castellina in Chianti, and at the Biological Market in Florence held the third Sunday of each month.

## DUCCIO'S AROMATIC HERBS

*Natural spontaneous growth and planned cultivation supply Duccio with a wide range of herbs to dry for his spice blends. These mixtures change from season to season, year to year, depending on his current harvest and his current whim. It is possible to create your own blends, too. Some suggestions have been made in the following recipes.*

| | | | |
|---|---|---|---|
| *aglio* | garlic | *origano* | oregano |
| *alloro* | bay | *ortica* | nettle |
| *basilico* | basil | *porro* | leek |
| *cipolla* | onion | *peperoncino piccante* | hot chile |
| *coriandolo* | coriander | *prezzemolo* | parsley |
| *dragoncello* | tarragon | *rafano* | horseradish |
| *elicriso* | licorice | *rosmarino* | rosemary |
| *erba cipollina* | chive | *ruta* | rue |
| *erba di San Pietro* | St. Peter's herb | *salvia* | sage |
| *finocchio* | fennel | *santoreggia* | summer savory |
| *ginepro* | juniper | *scalogno* | scallion |
| *issopo* | hyssop | *sedano* | celery |
| *lavanda* | lavendar | *senape* | mustard |
| *maggiorana* | marjoram | *timo* | thyme |
| *melissa* | melissa | *tanaceto* | tansy |
| *menta* | mint | *zafferano* | saffron |
| *nepitella* | calamint | | |

# INVOLTINI DI TACCHINO AGL'AROMI TOSCANI
*Stuffed Turkey with Tuscan Herbs*

Many of the butcher shops in Chianti offer meat dishes ready to cook. One of my favorites is a fillet of turkey stuffed with ground meats and wrapped in *pancetta*. This is my version, simply spiced with Duccio's herbs. To make your own blend, in a mortar, crush together ¾ teaspoon dried rosemary, ¼ teaspoon dried sage, and 1 teaspoon dried chives. If you use fresh herbs, triple the measurements.

*2 turkey breast fillets, about ½ pound each, skinned*

*Salt and freshly ground pepper to taste*

*6 tablespoons extra-virgin olive oil*

*3 leeks, white part only, julienned*

*¼ pound sweet Italian sausages, casings removed*

*½ cup dry white wine*

*1 cup chicken stock*

*¼ pound* pancetta, *thinly sliced*

*2 teaspoons aromi da cucina del Chianti: rosmarino (rosemary), salvia (sage), scalogno (scallion)*

*¾ pound spinach, coarsely chopped*

❧ Preheat an oven to 375°F. Lightly oil a shallow baking dish.

❧ One at a time, place the breast fillets between 2 sheets of plastic wrap. Using a meat tenderizer, pound to an even thickness of ½ inch. Season with salt and pepper. Set aside.

❧ In a large sauté pan over medium heat, warm 2 tablespoons of the olive oil. Add the leeks and sauté until softened, about 5 minutes. Add the sausage and cook until lightly browned, about 5 minutes longer. Pour in the wine and deglaze the pan, loosening the browned bits from the surface of the pan. Cook until reduced to a glaze, then add the chicken stock. Continue to reduce until slightly thickened, about 10 minutes longer. Drain through a sieve, reserving the liquid.

❧ Divide the leek-sausage mixture in half and spread evenly onto each turkey slice. Starting from a long side, roll up each slice. Wrap a piece of *pancetta* around the outside and secure with a toothpick or kitchen string.

❧ In a sauté pan over medium-high heat, warm 2 tablespoons of the olive oil. Add the turkey rolls and cook, turning as necessary, until lightly browned, about 2 minutes on each side. Transfer the rolls to the prepared baking dish, arranging them in a single layer. Spoon the reserved liquid over the top. Sprinkle with the herb mixture. Cover and bake until the rolls are firm to the touch, about 20 minutes.

❧ In a saucepan over medium heat, warm the remaining 2 tablespoons olive oil. Add the spinach, cover, and let wilt for 2 minutes. Uncover and season with salt and pepper. Transfer to a warmed serving platter and keep warm.

❧ Remove the toothpicks or string from the turkey rolls and cut crosswise into ½-inch-thick slices. Arrange on top of the spinach and serve at once.

*SERVES 4*

# ZUCCHINI COTTI AL FORNO

*Roasted Herbed Zucchini* ~ Duccio Fontani

The fennel flower, *fior di finocchio*, plays an important role as one of Tuscany's unique flavoring ingredients. At the end of summer, the tiny pollen-laden yellow blooms that grow in clusters are collected and dried. Sprinkled over roasted meats or vegetables, this herb has a sweet aroma and incomparable flavor. Near Siena, it is also used to coat *salame*, adding a wonderful contrast to the spiciness of the meat. You can make a substitute blend for this recipe using 1 teaspoon fennel flower, ¼ teaspoon dry mustard, and a pinch of cayenne pepper. Save the oil left in the baking pan after cooking the zucchini for adding to a salad dressing or for brushing on toasted bread.

Preheat an oven to 400°F. Lightly oil a baking sheet.

Bring a saucepan of salted water to a boil. Add the zucchini and blanch for 30 seconds. Drain and immerse immediately in ice water to stop the cooking. Drain again, pat dry, and place in a bowl. Add the olive oil and herb blend and toss well. Spread on the prepared baking sheet.

Bake until tender and lightly browned, 12 to 15 minutes. Remove from the oven, add the flowers, and toss well. Arrange on a serving platter, season with salt and pepper, and serve.

*SERVES 6*

*1 pound baby zucchini, trimmed*

*3 tablespoons extra-virgin olive oil*

*1½ teaspoons* aromi da cucina del Chianti: finocchio *(fennel flower),* senape *(mustard), and* peperoncino *(crushed chile)*

*A few zucchini flowers*

*Salt and freshly ground pepper to taste*

# SPIEDINI DI GAMBERI E PORCINI
*Grilled Shrimp and Porcini Mushrooms*

This recipe was inspired by a meal I had in Cinqueterre. The shrimp had been marinated in pesto, then grilled. Here I marinate them in Duccio's *aromi*, or you can prepare the following substitute: in a mortar, crush together ¼ teaspoon dry mustard, ½ teaspoon dried mint, and 1 teaspoon dried parsley, and blend with 1 clove garlic, finely minced. When fresh porcini are unavailable, substitute your favorite fresh local mushroom.

*18 jumbo shrimp or prawns, peeled
    and deveined*

*9 fresh porcini mushrooms, cut into quarters*

*36 chunks sweet red onion*

*¼ cup extra-virgin olive oil*

*2 teaspoons* aromi da cucina del Chianti:
    senape *(mustard)*, nepitella *(calamint)*,
    prezzemolo *(parsley)*, aglio *(garlic)*

*2 cloves garlic, minced*

*Salt and freshly ground pepper to taste*

❧ Thread 1 shrimp or prawn, 2 pieces porcini, and 2 pieces onion onto each skewer. Place in a shallow nonreactive dish.

❧ In a small bowl, whisk together the olive oil, herb blend, and garlic. Pour evenly over the skewers and allow to marinate for at least 1 hour at room temperature, or cover and refrigerate for as long as overnight.

❧ Prepare a fire in a grill, or preheat a broiler.

❧ Remove the skewers from the marinade, reserving the marinade, and season with salt and pepper. Place on the grill or in the broiler and grill or broil, turning frequently and brushing with the marinade, until the shellfish are pink, 4 to 5 minutes. Serve immediately.

*SERVES 6*

# COOKING FROM THE LAND
## Carlo Cioni, *Da Delfina*
### Artimino (Tuscany)

*It's my dear friend Rolando's birthday. What better place to celebrate but Da Delfina—perfectly Tuscan food in a perfectly Tuscan setting.*

*Artimino, May 1994*

Tuscany was the heart of the Renaissance in the fifteenth century. Its place at the crossroads of northern and southern trade, its fertile soil and wealth of natural products made it a center for commerce and art. Here, the great Dukes of Tuscany prospered. Of their many villas, the Villa La Ferdinanda, known as the *cento camini,* "one hundred chimneys," still stands in Artimino, a twenty-five-minute drive west of Florence. Under the Medici noble system, peasants whose work supported the royal lifestyle of *il populo grasso*, literally "the fat people," lived on tiny pieces of land or in the wild hills surrounding the homes of the nobles. These peasants foraged for food and developed cooking techniques to augment their meager existence.

In the shadow of La Ferdinanda's one hundred chimneys is a restaurant that pays tribute to *la cucina povera*, "the cooking of the peasants." Chef Carlo Cioni focuses his menu at Da Delfina on foods that have a history and seasonality. "Today's choice of simple foods is not out of necessity as in the past," says Carlo. "Now we are seeking quality and essence as opposed to extravagance." His cooking emphasizes the use of local, natural, and seasonal ingredients—ingredients that often send him out to forage on the hillsides near his restaurant. He reaches into the past to find natural ingredients and cooking methods that reward diners with simple, yet superb, dishes.

*Delfina and Carlo Cioni.*

Delfina is Carlo's mother. She opened the restaurant in its present location in 1976, after twenty years of cooking at the Paggeria Medicea, at one time the stables of the villa (now a four-star hotel). During that time, the villa was privately owned by a Venetian noble family and was a hunting lodge, open to the public. Delfina cooked for the tourists that visited. Her table was renowned, and when she established Da Delfina, she began training her son, Carlo, and a nephew to carry on the traditions of *i piatti della nonna,* that is, a grandmother's cooking. Today, at the dear age of ninety-two, she still cooks for the kitchen staff and can often be seen shelling beans or folding the laundry she hangs on the line twice a day. Carlo has taken on the tradition with great spirit and passion. "My goal is to keep with the original third- and fourth-generation recipes, adding some practical inventions while keeping the essence of the older styles. The cooking is based on family traditions, local geography, and the culture of the peasant."

Carlo's cooking is a study of *la cucina povera*. "Peasants cooked with parsimony, using spare amounts of condiments," he explains. "Spices were not available, so they gathered herbs to perfume their cuisine." Bread, for example, was expensive and therefore never wasted, thus the creation of a dish like *ribollita,* which utilizes an

*Many of Cioni's ingredients are from his garden or foraged from the surrounding hillsides.*

economy of cooking that maximizes everything to the last drop. This same cuisine could also be a rich one, for there has always been an abundance of fresh ingredients from the local gardens and surrounding countryside. "You develop a palate for the best time of the season for ingredients; for example, the flavor of nettles in February is different from the same plant in June. And the poppy flower and leaves from Abetone are exceptional in March."

Tuscans are known for their austerity and preference for the simple things, as a local proverb illustrates: *Si stava meglio quando si stava peggio—* "We were better off when we were worse off."

*Cioni emphasizes the use of seasonal, local ingredients.*

# SFORMATO DI ORTICHE
*Nettle Timbale* - Carlo Cioni

Nettles have many healthful properties, among them their use as an antidote for allergy problems. If you are unable to forage nettles in your area, substitute spinach.

*1 pound fava beans, shelled*
  *(about ½ pound shelled beans)*

*1⅓ pounds nettles*

*1 egg, lightly beaten*

*½ cup milk*

*6 tablespoons extra-virgin olive oil*

*1 teaspoon minced fresh rosemary*

*1 teaspoon minced fresh sage*

*1 clove garlic, minced*

*1 ripe tomato, passed through a food mill*
  *or sieve*

✎ Bring a saucepan of water to a boil. Add the fava beans, reduce the heat to medium, and cook until tender, about 20 minutes. Drain and pass through a food mill. Alternatively, slip the beans from their skins and puree them in a food processor. Set aside.

✎ Preheat an oven to 350°F. Lightly butter four 6-ounce ramekins.

✎ Bring a saucepan of water to a boil. Add the nettles and cook until tender, about 3 minutes. Drain and squeeze out as much water as possible. Pass them through a food mill or puree in a food processor. Return the nettles to the saucepan and cook over low heat until all the moisture is evaporated. Set aside to cool.

✎ Add the egg and milk to the cooled nettles, mixing well, then divide among the prepared ramekins. Place the ramekins in a large baking pan and add hot water to reach halfway up the sides of the ramekins.

✎ Carefully place the pan in the oven and bake until a knife inserted in the center of a ramekin comes out clean, 55 to 60 minutes.

✎ Meanwhile, in a sauté pan over medium heat, warm the olive oil. Add the rosemary, sage, and garlic and sauté until softened but not browned, 2 to 3 minutes. Add the puree of tomato and the favas and cook over low heat until smooth and thickened, about 30 minutes.

✎ Divide the bean puree among 4 individual plates. Loosen the edges of each ramekin with a knife and invert onto a pool of the bean puree. Serve at once.

*SERVES 4*

# RIBOLLITA DI CAMPAGNA

*Country-Style* Ribollita ~ Carlo Cioni

*Ribollita*, literally "reboiled," is a traditional Tuscan dish that exemplifies the frugality and resourcefulness of local cooks in using leftover ingredients. Carlo insists it must be made on top of the stove, not in the oven, a version often seen in restaurants. Oil is used sparingly, preciously, even as a garnish, for this is a peasant dish.

**Day One**

## MINESTRA DI VERDURA

*Vegetable Soup*

Sixty percent of this soup is cabbage, primarily the kale-like *cavolo nero*. Carlo admonishes cooks to handle the beans tenderly and cook them slowly and *dolcemente*, "sweetly," so they are not bruised. He soaks them overnight with aromatics: whole cloves of garlic, a bay leaf, and a sprig of sage. Use any seasonal vegetables in this dish, and cook them in the order of hardness. Start with such items as potatoes, which take longer to cook, and finish with the tender herbs.

❧ In a large pot over medium heat, warm the olive oil. Add the onion, carrots, and celery and sauté until golden, about 3 minutes. Add the garlic and stock and bring to a boil. Now reduce the heat to low and begin adding the vegetables—*cavolo nero* or kale, potatoes, leafy greens, aromatic greens, and zucchini—adding those that take the longest to cook first until they begin to soften before you add the next ingredient. When all of them are tender, add the white beans and aromatic herbs. Continue to simmer for about 20 minutes, being careful not to over-cook the beans.

❧ Season to taste with salt and pepper and ladle into bowls to serve.

*2 tablespoons extra-virgin olive oil*

*1 onion, diced*

*2 carrots, peeled and diced*

*1 celery stalk, diced*

*2 cloves garlic, minced*

*2½ quarts vegetable stock*

*4 cups shredded* cavolo nero *or kale*

*1 or 2 potatoes, peeled and cubed*

*1 cup shredded assorted leafy greens such as Swiss chard, nettles, and spinach*

*1 cup coarsely chopped assorted aromatic greens such as borage, fennel, and mustard*

*3 zucchini, trimmed and coarsely chopped*

*2 cups cooked and drained white beans*

*¼ cup minced assorted fresh aromatic herbs such as parsley, rosemary, and sage*

*Salt and freshly ground pepper to taste*

## Day Two
### MINESTRA DI PANE
*Bread Soup*

*Country-style bread*
*Extra-virgin olive oil*

Reheat the leftover soup. Place very thin slices of country-style bread on the bottom of a lightly oiled baking dish. Spoon one-third of the warm soup over the bread and repeat with two more layers of bread and soup. Cover and let stand for 15 minutes in a warm place before serving.

## Day Three
### MINESTRA DI PANE
*Bread Soup*

*Diced onion*
*Extra-virgin olive oil*

Sprinkle diced onion over the leftover bread and soup in the baking dish and drizzle with extra-virgin olive oil (always scant). Bake in a 375°F oven until the onions are lightly browned and mixture is warmed through, about 20 minutes.

## Day Four
### RIBOLLITA
*Tuscan Bread and Vegetable Soup*

*Extra-virgin olive oil*
*Freshly ground pepper to taste*

Lightly brush a skillet with olive oil. Spoon the remaining *minestra di pane* into the pan and brown over medium heat until crispy on the bottom, 4 to 5 minutes. Turn and crisp the other side. Garnish with a little extra-virgin olive oil and freshly ground pepper. The *ribollita* should be firm enough to eat with a fork.

# CONIGLIO IN UMIDO CON GALLETTI

**Braised Rabbit with Chanterelles** ~ Carlo Cioni

On a sunny spring day, just after a rain, the hillsides offer the gift of *galletti,* tender chanterelle mushrooms. This is when peasants live like kings. Serve this tender rabbit over little mounds of creamy polenta (see recipe, page 39), spooning some of the pan juices over the top.

❧ In a large, wide pot over medium heat, warm the olive oil. Add the rabbit, onion, garlic, rosemary, and wine and cook, uncovered, until the liquid evaporates, 15 to 20 minutes. Add the tomato puree, mushrooms, and stock and bring to a boil. Reduce the heat to a steady simmer and cook, uncovered, until the rabbit is tender and the sauce has thickened slightly, about 15 minutes.

❧ Transfer to a serving bowl and serve immediately.

*SERVES 4*

*3 tablespoons extra-virgin olive oil*

*1 rabbit, about 3 pounds,*
*    cut into 8 serving pieces*

*½ onion, diced*

*3 cloves garlic, minced*

*1 fresh rosemary sprig*

*1 cup dry white wine*

*2 ripe tomatoes, passed through a food mill*
*    or sieve*

*¾ pound fresh chanterelle mushrooms*

*1 cup chicken stock*

# FARAONA AL VIN SANTO COTTA AL FORNO

*Roasted Guinea Hen in* Vin Santo - Carlo Cioni

The original recipe for this dish came from a journal that dates back to 1815, one of Carlo's resources for the historical methods he uses in the restaurant. The ingredients are simple and rely on seasonality and freshness to flavor the guinea hen. Local products are featured in the dish, such as *vin santo* (see description on page 160) and herbs and spices that have been foraged from the nearby hills.

*1 guinea hen, about 2 pounds,*
*cut in half lengthwise*

*2 bay leaves*

*3 tablespoons extra-virgin olive oil*

*5 fresh sage leaves*

*1 teaspoon juniper berries*

*Salt and freshly ground pepper to taste*

*1 cup vin santo*

*1 lemon zest strip, ½ inch wide*

℘ Position an oven rack in the upper third of an oven and preheat to 375°F. Lightly butter a medium-sized roasting pan.

℘ Loosen the skin on the breast of each guinea hen half with your fingers and tuck a bay leaf under it. Place the hen halves in the prepared roasting pan skin side up. Sprinkle with the olive oil, sage, juniper berries, salt, and pepper.

℘ Place on the upper rack in the oven and roast until lightly browned, 20 to 30 minutes. Remove from the oven and add the *vin santo* and lemon zest to the pan. Return to the oven and roast until tender, turning occasionally to brown the meat on all sides, about 15 minutes longer.

℘ Arrange on a warmed platter or individual plates. Drizzle with the pan juices and serve at once.

SERVES 2

# V

## MEATS

### CURED GAME
Bossi & Turchi

*Typical regional* salumi

### CULATELLO
Massimo Spigaroli

*Chianina beef*

### GAME
Iacopo Biondi Santi

*Culatello of Zibello is produced only in a tiny area of Emilia-Romagna.*

# MEATS

In these times of relative plenty, meat seems to be an essential component of the Italian table, but it hasn't always been so. Today the second course, offered after the pasta (or rice or soup) course, often features beef, veal, pork, poultry, or game. Hunting is still a great sport and, in some cases, a means of survival. In the fall, the choices of game are many—duck, songbirds such as thrush and lark, pheasant, quail, squab, hare, boar, and venison—the products of hunters' outings in the wilder parts of Italy or of purchases in open-air markets in its tamer regions. The meat of many of these wild animals is also cured.

In general, cured Italian meats are called salumi, *which include ground meat mixtures in casings, such as* salsicce, salami, *and salted air-dried meats such as* capocollo, prosciutto, *and* pancetta. *Although typically made from pork, some, such as* bresaola, *are made from beef and sometimes horse. Pliny the Elder, a first-century Italian historian, summed up the preference for pork when he said, "From no other animal can man draw more material for gluttony: pork has almost fifty different flavors, whereas other animals have only one."*

Each region has its own local specialty, plus most have a version of the more common treatments, such as coppa, *a peppery blend of pork head and shoulder, and* spalla, *pork shoulder cured in a similar manner to that for prosciutto. What differs from area to area is the blend of spices and seasonings. The amounts of salt and pepper vary greatly, along with the variety of flavorings, which may include everything from cinnamon, cloves, coriander, and fennel seeds to garlic, mace, nutmeg, and* peperoncino *(chile). Fennel, for example, is found primarily in central Italy, while spicy* peperoncini *are more popular in the south.*

Prosciutto di Parma *is a perfect example of a product that has been industrialized yet maintains its quality. All aspects of manufacture, from the breeding of the pigs and their care to the packaging of the end product, are rigidly controlled by the* Istituto Parma Qualità (IPQ). *The yearly quota of eight million* prosciutti *comes from just over two hundred producers. The source of these* prosciutti *is four million pigs, most from a breed called Large White, which originated in the Bourbon court in Naples in the early nineteenth century. A cross between a Neapolitan pig and an English pig, each of these tasty animals weighs in at over three hundred pounds. They are raised on some six thousand pig farms near Parma.*

*The prosciutto is the whole back leg of the animal with the bone in. The salt-curing phase lasts for two months, the leg rinsed and massaged with fresh salt every few weeks. After that, the meat is washed in warm water, dried, trimmed, and shaped. It is aged for ten to twelve months, during which it is hung in cool temperatures. The minimum weight for a finished prosciutto is just over fifteen pounds. A consortium-approved prosciutto includes a distinctive trademarked brand: Parma, in capital letters, in a crown.*

*Perhaps the most precious of the* salumi *is the* culatello, *a cut that comes from the fleshy posterior of the pig. Writer Folco Portinari, perhaps best known as the father of Dante's lover, talks about the name* culatello, *literally "little buttocks." "During our childhood, in my generation, pronouncing it* [culatello] *in the 'good' rooms of our house was forbidden, so we repeated that name softly, almost as a secret, like among conspirators of a secret sect; forced the rest of the time to play around it with euphemisms, which devalued its imposing strength, regal splendor, and musical expressiveness."*

*What makes* culatello *so special is the hands-on method of preparation and the foggy climate natural to the tiny pocket of Emilia-Romagna where it is made. This moist environment encourages mold to grow on the walls of the ancient stone aging rooms where the* culatello *is hung, the mold acting as an essential component in the development of the cured meat's unique flavor. Imagine the reaction of government sanitation inspectors. There was, in fact, quite a struggle in getting the process to comply with industrial standards.*

# CURED GAME
## Bossi & Turchi
### Rigomagno Scalo (Tuscany)

*I can't believe I have still never seen a live wild boar. Tonight, since they are nocturnal animals, I drove my car into the woods, turned off the lights, and sat there waiting for some to cross the moonlit road. It didn't happen.*

*Gaiole in Chianti, May 1996*

As much as I love *prosciutto di Parma,* I have to admit I'm partial to the prosciutto of Tuscany—it is sweet and dense, and much saltier than its Parma counterpart. And I'm especially fond of prosciutto made from wild boar, somewhat of a rarity. I was quite surprised to learn of a business that is actually producing five thousand of them each year.

When I arrived at Bossi & Turchi, in Rigomagno Scalo, just outside of Sinalunga in the province of Siena, I was more than a little skeptical, especially when I was made to don a lab coat and surgical room slippers to take a tour of the facility. The company was founded in the early sixties by Giorgio Bossi and Gino Turchi. Both come from families of butchers that specialize in game. For twenty years, they had continued their family traditions in Castelnuova Berardenga, a tiny village near Siena. When they moved to Rigomagno Scalo in the late eighties, they took the opportunity to modernize the business. It was in their best interest to do so, because it was not long before the European Union (EU) began imposing stringent hygienic controls on producers of cured meats. Bossi &

*Prosciutto aging.*

Turchi strive to maintain the traditional methods within these strictures, a particular challenge with raw cured hams such as prosciutto.

I was impressed. Against a backdrop of white tiles and chalkboards lined with sanitation schedules, there persisted an inherent quality in the work. The juniper, *peperoncino* (chile), and bay used to cure the prosciutto are all natural and of high quality. The leg of the boar, its hairy skin intact, is massaged and marinated with wine, salt, and spices for twenty days. It then airs for forty days, ages in cool refrigeration for another forty, and finally moves to a warm room to finish, for a total of six months. At the end, the prosciutto usually weighs around eleven pounds. Bossi & Turchi also produces deer prosciutto, turkey *bresaola, salumi* of wild boar, goose, and roe-deer, as well as pork *coppa.* For one of my favorite *salumi, finocchiona,* a *salame* coated with the seeds and flowers of the wild fennel plant, the company has selected the Cinta Senese, an old breed of pig that is also prized for use in Tuscan-style prosciutto.

# TYPICAL REGIONAL *SALUMI*

*The ultimate way to serve cured meats is uncooked, usually as an antipasto. A sliced assortment, called* affettato misto, *is best accompanied by a simple complement of sliced cheeses and fresh fig or ripe melon. Wrap prosciutto around breadsticks (see* Grissini, *page 45) and serve it with vegetables, fresh or preserved in oil or vinegar. A simple loaf of country bread and olive oil are also pleasing with* salumi, *as is a glass of chilled dry white wine.*

*Some cured meats do lend themselves well to cooking. Prosciutto in small amounts adds flavor to soups, risottos, pasta, and vegetables. See* I Leccabaffi *(page 70) and* Timballo di Maccheroni *(page 54) for two examples. Pancetta is used much like bacon, wrapped around meats or browned and crumbled into creamy dishes. Two examples are found in* Involtini di Tacchino agl'Aromi Toscani *(page 97) and* Pane Santo *(page 20).*

*Below are some regional specialties you should be sure to try when you are in Italy.*

**ABRUZZO**
Capelomme – *pork fillet, smoked and aged*

**APULIA**
Salsicce leccese – *veal and pork sausage seasoned with lemon peel and cinnamon*

**BASILICATA**
Lucanica – *spicy pork sausage*

**CALABRIA**
'Nduja – *soft, spicy sausage of ground meats, fat, liver, and lungs*

**CAMPANIA**
Salame napoletana – *ground pork and beef* salame *seasoned with pepper and garlic*

**EMILIA-ROMAGNA**
Capello da prete– salame *in triangular "priest's hat"*
Culatello – *pork rump salt-cured in a pig's bladder*
Mortadella – *Bolognese pork sausage*
Prosciutto di Parma
Zampone – *pork sausage stuffed in a pig's trotter*

**LAZIO**
Guanciale – *pork cheek cured with salt and pepper*
Scammarita – *pork neck cured with salt, pepper, and wild fennel*

**LIGURIA**
Salame di Sant'Olcese – *pork and beef, smoked and aged*

**LOMBARDY**
Bresaola – *beef fillet, salted and air-dried*
Luganega – *spicy coiled sausage*
Violino – *prosciutto of goat*

**MARCHES**
Musetto – *boiled* salame

**MOLISE**
Mulette – *spicy* capocollo *(neck)*

**PIEDMONT**
Salame al Barolo – *long, soft* salame *flavored with Barolo*
Salamin d'la duja – *pork* salame *aged in ceramic under rendered pork fat*

**SARDINIA**
Lingua – *brined pork or lamb tongue*

**SICILY**
Soppressata – *pressed spicy* salame

**TOSCANA**
Finocchiona – *soft pork* salame *with wild fennel seeds*
Finocchiata – *pork shoulder and neck (capocollo) cured in pepper and wild fennel seeds*
Lardo di Colonnata – *cured pork fat*
Prosciutto – cinghiale *(boar),* pork, cervo *(venison),* or daino *(roe deer)*

**TRE VENEZIE**
Kaminwürzen – *small smoked sausage*
Prosciutto di San Daniele
Soppressa – *large, soft* salame
Speck tirolese – *smoked prosciutto*

**UMBRIA**
Mazzafegati – *sweet sausage of pork liver, pine nuts, orange peel, raisins, and sugar*

**VAL D'AOSTA**
Lardo – *cured pork fat*

# CULATELLO
## Massimo Spigaroli
### Polesine Parmense (Emilia-Romagna)

*That morning I told him we were going to a restaurant famous for* culatello. *"Do you know what* culatello *is?" He answered, "It's a cheese, right?" So I explained that, no, it is a special cured meat, taken from the rump of a pig; that a prosciutto is sacrificed to make it. "Oh yes," he said, nodding, "I'm sure I've had that before . . . I think in Venice." And so I said probably not, because it is only made in this one tiny area of Emilia-Romagna. After lunch, he announced that it was the best* culatello *he'd ever had!*

*Polesine Parmense, May 1998*

In 1920, the Spigaroli family had a small boat they used to ferry passengers and commodities across the Po River at Polesine Parmense, a small village northwest of Parma. To make the wait for the little boat more comfortable, the family created a park with trees and flowers and opened a small *osteria* called Lido. In time, people came just to enjoy a meal of fresh river fish and eel cooked by the women of the family. The diners were also treated to house-made *culatello* and *salame*.

The restaurant closed during the war and remained closed for some time. But Massimo's father, Marcello, his mother, Enrica, and his Aunt Emilia re-established and refurbished the business in 1960, transforming it from a riverside *osteria* into a proper restaurant called Al Cavallino Bianco (The Little White Horse). At this time, Massimo was a toddler, and as he grew up he spent a lot of time in the kitchen watching his aunt work her mastery with the food and helping when possible.

When he was old enough, Massimo began his formal training at the hotel school in nearby Salsomaggiore, and later worked in five-star hotels and restaurants all over the world. When he returned to Polesine Parmense, he took charge of the kitchen and production on the family farm, and of the curing of the *salumi*.

*Massimo Spigaroli.*

Massimo's father and grandfather were farmers. From them he learned the importance of completely natural products, one of the reasons the restaurant maintained such a good reputation. The local pigs, cattle, sheep, poultry, honey, vegetables, and fruits all guarantee the restaurant a pantry of premium-quality ingredients. But the prime offering, and perhaps the original reason the restaurant became such a destination for diners, was the *culatello*.

This unique commodity has a legacy that can be traced back to the 1300s. It comes from the same part of the pig as prosciutto, the back leg, but only the butt is used for *culatello*. When this cut is removed, it is no longer possible to create a prosciutto. Of course, the excess meat is used for other types of *salumi*, but the producer must reckon the value of the *culatello* versus a prosciutto. Economically, it seems to work out: the *culatello* brings a price three times higher per kilo (a little over two pounds) than prosciutto does, and it is roughly one-third the weight in yield.

*Culatello* can only be produced in a small area called the Bassa Parmense. It is bordered by the Po River and stretches slightly south to the tangent rivers Taro and Ongina. Eight communities are permitted to

## CHIANINA BEEF

*The best steak in Italy is from a young indigenous white cow called* Chianina, *raised primarily in the Val di Chiana, which spans Tuscany and Umbria. One of the oldest breeds of cattle in existence, it is becoming increasingly rare in butcher shops. A consortium called* Cinque Razze *(Five Races), formed to verify the authenticity of several native breeds, guarantees that the consumer is not buying imported or hormone-treated meat. In addition to the Chianina, the protected breeds include the Podolica, the cow used for caciocavallo cheese (see chapter three), the Maremmana, which is known for its excellent drinking milk, the Marchigiana from the Marches, and the northern Romagnola.*

*In Tuscany and Umbria, menus use the term* bistecca di fiorentina *for Chianina steak, and if it is truly from the Chianina, the price is dear, charged by weight. Up to two inches thick and weighing about two pounds, it should be grilled quickly on both sides over hot wood coals until the outside is seared and the inside is quite rare, only three to four minutes on each side. After that, it is seasoned only with salt, pepper, and freshly milled extra-virgin olive oil. It is often served topped with shredded arugula or spinach, with some tender* cannellini *beans alongside.*

make what is legally named *culatello di Zibello*: Busseto, Polesine Parmenese, Zibello, Soragna, Roccabianca, San Secondo, Sissa, and Colorno. The first registered trademark was in Zibello, and the name stuck when the *denominazione di origine protetta* (DOP), the protection of the area of production, was defined to include the other areas.

This tiny zone, smaller than seventy-five square miles, has several unique properties that give *culatello* its individual character. The essential factor is constant humidity. These are lowlands that border rivers, which, in the autumn, swim in a dense fog. Fog is fundamental to the maturation and aging of *culatello*. In addition, dampness from the rivers and the high moisture content in the soil maintain the humidity throughout the cold winters and sunny summers.

The moist aging rooms of stone and brick hold airborne molds that encourage this meat to greatness. As a result, traditional *culatello* came into danger when the local health and sanitation department in conjunction with new European Union standards began to demand sanitary conditions in the curing process. Many producers went underground. Some decided to create an industrial product made under sterile conditions that satisfied the law, but not the palates of the cognoscenti.

Through intense lobbying by some of the producers, the consortium for *culatello di Zibello* came about in October 1996, when the zone was finally granted DOP standing. Leading the initiative was Massimo Spigaroli, now president of the consortium. Twelve producers from the area adhere to strict controls and regulations regarding the traditional process of handling and curing the meat, and its origins and treatment prior to butchering. The consortium inspects and approves each *culatello* after eleven months of aging. If it passes the inspection, it receives the trademark for *culatello di Zibello*.

Across the narrow road in front of Al Cavallino Bianco is a stone house originally built in the 1600s. The simple wooden doors do not hold a clue to the riches inside: hundreds of Massimo's *salumi* hang drying from wooden rafters and racks, among them a great number of *culatelli*. The floor is brick and the walls are plaster, multihued with years of beneficial microbes and molds. In the dim light, a narrow stair leads up to the attic, where more meats hang, filling the entire space. In each room there is a small window, usually closed. "We open a window to let in the moisture of a fog or the heat of a summer day, but we are careful not to allow a draft to circulate too much," explains Massimo. Even so, the air is not at all musty. A sweet aroma lingers.

Massimo explains how the *culatello* is made. It starts with their own hogs, raised on a wholesome diet. The babies are fed *latticello*, whey left over from cheese making, until they weigh about fifty pounds. After that they eat

*The moist aging rooms hold airborne molds that encourage*
culatello *to greatness.*

half). The first stage occurs over the winter and is cool and slow. It helps form the superficial crust, which maintains moistness inside. The actual temperature is determined by natural forces, although the ideal is 57° to 64°F, with 75 to 85 percent humidity. After eleven months, an impartial inspector from the consortium will test the *culatello*. He inserts a *gugia*, a probe made of horse bone, and checks the aroma for any problems. A finished product will range in size from five and a half to thirteen pounds, depending on the size of the pig. It reduces in size by 40 percent after twelve months of aging.

Industrial producers can make *culatello* year-round by artificially controlling the humidity and temperature. Most of the work is done under refrigeration in rooms lined with ceramic tiles. The law for the industrial products allows the use of potassium nitrate (saltpeter), a preservative. In *Treasures of the Italian Table*, Burton Anderson says, "Some examples might be tasty, but, as they say, the real thing is the 'caviar of the Bassa,' the other stuff is fish eggs."

Massimo reminds me that *culatello* is a "cultural" product, the traditions handed down by families for generations. Next to the restaurant, he has a bar-*caffè* that opens onto a casual trattoria. One wall is devoted to gastronomic merchandise, for discriminating cooks. In front of these offerings is a marble-and-wood bar recovered from a *drogheria* and restored. Massimo points out the prominent pig's head carved into the wood, saying, "This just shows how important the pig is in this region."

Massimo is a quiet man, at home in the elegant but warm dining room with its antique furnishings and large blazing fireplace. Of course the menu features *il nostro culatello*, his sweet and delicate homemade *culatello*, served with the soft local bread called *micca*. The river provides a number of freshwater catches, from catfish to frog's legs to eel, dishes that harken back to the restaurant's origins, when hungry fishermen would cross the river to taste the cooking of Massimo's aunt.

corn, *grana farina* (flour), and barley, along with bread and vegetable scraps from the restaurant.

The work begins in November. Immediately after butchering, the meat is portioned and the skin and bone removed. The *culatello* is covered with salt and some other spices and seasonings. Each producer makes his own blend, which may include whole pepper and sometimes garlic. The salt is 3.3 percent of the weight of the meat, but is measured only by "eye and experience." The spice mixture is massaged energetically into the flesh, which is then left to rest for six to ten days. Every two or three days, the *culatello* is massaged, soaked in white wine, and salted again, continually pressed and formed into its classic pear shape. After salting and shaping, the *culatello* is stitched into the bladder of the pig and artfully woven with a running knot to help maintain the pear shape.

The *culatello* spends the next eleven to fifteen months aging (larger butts may take up to a year and a

# GAME
## Iacopo Biondi Santi
### Montalcino (Tuscany)

*Anna brought us to her family trattoria, La Casa di Caccia, in the mountains. We were surrounded by tables of men who she told us were eating the game they had shot a few days ago. They come to hunt for the sport of it, return a few days later after the meat has aged, and the cook prepares a meal to order.*

*Mugello, November 1995*

November first is *Ognissanti,* All Saints' Day, a time to pay homage to saints and a day when families gather to remember those who have passed on. It is also the opening day of the hunting season for wild boar. Suddenly the roads are full of cars pulling small trailers carrying yelping dogs. The pop of gunfire resounds through the hills. Hunters, breath steaming from the cold, stomp across the land behind the dogs as they trail the gnarly boar.

One such hunter is Iacopo Biondi Santi. This handsome man looks equally at home in the down, flannel, and corduroy uniform of the hunter as he does in his stylish Italian suits. His vocation is wine making; his passion is hunting.

Six generations of Biondi Santi's began when Clemente Santi, with his daughter Caterina, began cultivating and carefully selecting the Sangiovese Grosso grape. Caterina married Jacopo Biondi and continued to develop the business with their son, Ferruccio. In the late 1800s, Ferruccio created the magnificent Brunello di Montalcino from the Sangiovese Grosso grape, a rich red wine that spends at least four years in oak. For the last twenty-five years, Ferruccio's sons, Tancredi and Franco, have brought world recognition to Brunello. Iacopo, Franco's son, carries on the tradition,

*Iacopo Biondi Santi.*

adding his own contribution of highly rated Super-Tuscans and classic wines from the family merger with Poggio Salvi, the estate of his wife, Francesca.

The first time I met Iacopo and Francesca was at a dinner offered in their home just outside of Montalcino. I arrived by a winding road through the vineyards, welcomed by the barking of Iacopo's large white hunting dog. Inside the house, my first impression was of walls filled with hunting trophies, heads and racks of the rugged little *capriolo* (fallow deer) and majestic *daino* (roe deer). Francesca laughed, "We will need to build another house soon just to hold Iacopo's mementos."

Dinner was the hunter's catch. Iacopo did most of the cooking, including a stew of *capriolo* simmered with red wine and herbs for eight hours in a pot made by hand in Valtellino of *pietra ollare,* a stone resistant to fire. On this crisp fall day, the weather, the food, and the wine worked together to create a classic picture of comfort: meats roasted over a crackling fire, fresh peppery olive oil drizzled over grilled Tuscan bread, the noble Brunello, and lively conversation.

Iacopo told us that due to its popularity, some boar is now raised for consumption. Hunting is a way of controlling the population of these pesky creatures, who are known to ravage gardens in their nightly forays. "In the wild, the dew claw is developed, whereas the domestic animals have none," he explained. The boar are often hunted *in battuta a posta*, a practice in which thirty to fifty men with thirty or so dogs station themselves in a circle around where the boars are hiding and beat the ground with sticks, making enough noise to flush the animals out.

"My earliest memory of hunting was my fascination with my grandparents' fantastic collection of weapons. My grandmother took me on my first hunting trip when I was six years old. I shot a sparrow, not a catch to be proud of," Iacopo recalls. "We hunted for our dinner, and there was no law governing what we could shoot, or when."

*Pheasant roam wild throughout Tuscany.*

Ten years ago, changes in the law imposed new restrictions on hunting. In order to get a license, one now needs to fill out numerous papers and comply with the rules. Hunting courses are offered to certify that applicants know the restrictions. "The idea could be positive, if it helped improve problems with poisoning of agriculture or protection of scarce animals," says Iacopo. "But it has just produced a paper bureaucracy—a way to create new jobs. The system is too complicated. It encourages hunters to go underground or not to hunt."

While a few wild animal populations are shrinking, some are still abundant and cause a certain nuisance. "The deer eat the grapes," Iacopo says. "The *daino* can eat twenty-five kilos [about fifty-five pounds] a day." But even to protect his crops a man must hunt only in the specified season and account for every animal he bags.

Upon receiving authorization to hunt, one is obliged to take a certain number of animals. The heads are brought to the area warden to be tagged, and other information about the animal is recorded, whether young or old, male or female. The heads must be kept in the freezer the entire season.

There are two ways to get permission to hunt: either with a *banda bianca*, the white band for landowners and their guests on private land, or the *banda rossa*, the red band that grants permission to hunt on a private *riserva*. Iacopo is the area warden for a nearby private reserve at Lucignano d'Asso, part of the old Piccolomini estate. He works year-round to cultivate the land with natural foods that will encourage wild animals to return and, in the hunting season, monitors the game that is taken.

His family eats everything Iacopo shoots. Throughout the year the game can be quite diverse. From the first of August to the nineteenth of September is the season for *daini, caprioli,* and *muflone* (wild sheep). From the nineteenth of September to the end of December nonmigratory game such as rabbit, pheasant, and partridge are in season, extending to the end of January for *tordi* (thrush), and *colombaccio* (wild pigeon). And wild boar season runs from the first of November until the end of January.

Iacopo learned the trade of butchering from a *norcino,* a local butcher, and does all of his own cleaning and cutting of the game. In the past, the game was hung to age for days, or even weeks. "When I was a child, I remember the horror of watching my father's game birds dessicate," Francesca recalls. "It smelled terrible and looked worse. I wouldn't eat it." Now she and Iacopo tenderize the meat by freezing it. It hangs for twelve hours or so, depending on the temperature, just to let the muscles relax, then is put into the freezer until ready to use.

Iacopo says, "My favorite way to cook deer or boar is the simplest. I like to season it with rosemary, sage, and garlic and let it roast slowly on the *girarrosto* [rotisserie]."

# RAGÙ DI CINGHIALE
*Wild Boar Sauce*

In the fall, the Tuscan hills resonate with the din of barking dogs and the echo of gunshots. Nearly every trattoria offers pasta served with a hearty sauce of long-simmered wild boar. Salty and rich, it makes a warm and satisfying first course. This recipe yields enough *ragù* to sauce about two pounds of pasta, preferably fettuccine. See Resources (page 163) for a source for ordering boar by mail, or substitute your choice of ground meats.

*3 tablespoons extra-virgin olive oil*

*1 onion, diced*

*2 carrots, peeled and diced*

*2 celery stalks, diced*

*1 pound boneless wild boar, coarsely ground*

*1 cup full-bodied red wine*

*2 cloves garlic, minced*

*1 tablespoon minced fresh rosemary*

*1 tablespoon minced fresh flat-leaf parsley*

*1 teaspoon minced fresh sage*

*1½ pounds tomatoes, peeled and coarsely chopped*

*Salt and freshly ground pepper to taste*

❧ In a large skillet over medium-high heat, warm the olive oil. Add the onion, carrot, and celery and sauté until golden brown, 3 to 4 minutes. Add the ground meat to the pan and cook, stirring, until the mixture is golden brown, 5 to 7 minutes. Add the wine and deglaze the pan, loosening the browned bits from the surface of the pan. Add the garlic, rosemary, parsley, sage, and tomatoes and stir well.

❧ Reduce the heat to low, cover, and cook until slightly thickened, about 1½ hours. Season with salt and pepper before serving.

*MAKES ABOUT 6 CUPS; SERVES 8*

# LEPRE BRASATO AL VINO BIANCO CON PATATE ARROSTO
## Hare Stewed in White Wine with Roasted Potatoes

Wild rabbit, *lepre*, is leaner than its domestic kin available in markets. Marinating it and then simmering it slowly helps tenderize the meat. Agrumato is an olive oil that is pressed with fresh oranges (see Resources, page 163). You can substitute extra-virgin olive oil and the minced zest of an orange.

To prepare the rabbit, place the pieces in a large, shallow non-reactive dish. In a small bowl, combine the ½ cup agramato olive oil, ½ cup of the wine, the rosemary, garlic, salt, and pepper. Pour over the rabbit and toss to coat well. Cover and marinate in the refrigerator for at least 8 hours or as long as overnight. Turn the pieces occasionally to ensure contact with the marinade.

Preheat an oven to 450°F.

In a large sauté pan over medium heat, heat the 3 tablespoons olive oil. Add the rabbit pieces, reserving the marinade, and cook, turning as needed, until golden brown on all sides, 5 to 7 minutes. Add the remaining 1 cup wine and ¼ cup of the reserved marinade. Reduce the heat to a simmer, cover, and cook until the rabbit is just tender, 20 to 25 minutes.

Meanwhile, prepare the potatoes: in a large bowl, toss the potatoes with the ¼ cup olive oil. Season with the rosemary, salt, and pepper and spread in an even layer in a roasting pan. Roast, turning occasionally, until the potatoes are golden brown, 30 to 40 minutes. Transfer to a serving platter and keep warm.

Uncover the rabbit and reduce the liquid over high heat until slightly thickened, 10 to 15 minutes longer. Season with salt and pepper. Transfer to a serving platter and serve at once with the potatoes.

*SERVES 4*

**For the rabbit:**

*1 rabbit, about 3 pounds, cut into 8 serving pieces*

*½ cup agrumato olive oil*

*1½ cups dry white wine*

*1 tablespoon minced fresh rosemary*

*3 cloves garlic, minced*

*Salt and freshly ground pepper to taste*

*3 tablespoons extra-virgin olive oil*

**For the potatoes:**

*2 pounds potatoes, cut into 2-inch chunks*

*¼ cup extra-virgin olive oil*

*1 tablespoon minced fresh rosemary*

*Salt and freshly ground pepper to taste*

# SPIEDINI DI UCCELLINI CON FINOCCHIONA

*Spit-Roasted Game Birds and* Finocchiona

Some of my favorite Italian meals have been made by the women cooks at La Bussola, a trattoria outside of Florence. One such meal was on a cold October night, warmed by fire-roasted birds and sausage paired with the local Carmignano wine. *Finocchiona* is a Tuscan sausage flavored with fennel seeds. Any fresh sausage can be used in its place. Serve these roasted meats over a mound of polenta (see recipe, page 39).

*6 pounds small birds such as thrush, squab, quail, or partridge*

*1 cup extra-virgin olive oil*

*1 cup full-bodied red wine*

*4 cloves garlic, minced*

*1 tablespoon juniper berries, crushed*

*1 teaspoon minced fresh rosemary*

*Salt and freshly ground pepper to taste*

*1 pound* finocchiona, *cut into 3-inch chunks*

❧ Place the birds in a shallow nonreactive dish. Leave small birds such as quail whole, and cut larger birds into equal-sized portions. In a small bowl, combine the olive oil, wine, garlic, juniper berries, rosemary, salt, and pepper. Pour over the birds and toss to coat well. Cover and marinate in the refrigerator for at least 8 hours or as long as overnight. Turn the birds occasionally to ensure contact with the marinade.

❧ Prepare a fire in a rotisserie. Remove the birds from the marinade, reserving the marinade, and skewer them on the spit, alternating the birds with pieces of sausage. Cook over the open fire, basting with the marinade, until the birds are tender, 12 to 15 minutes.

❧ Arrange the roasted birds and sausage pieces on a serving platter and serve at once.

*SERVES 4*

# VI

## RICE AND PASTA

**RICE**
Contessa Rosetta Clara Cavalli d'Olivola

**DRY PASTA**
Gianluigi Peduzzi

**FRESH PASTA**
Laura Galli, *Hosteria Giusti*

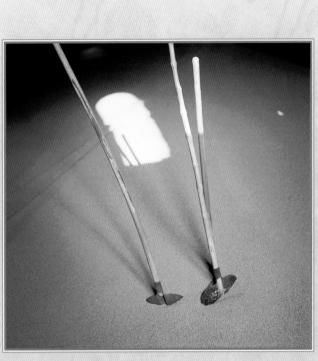

*A mountain of rice awaits processing.*

# RICE AND PASTA

*Risotto and pasta. Americans often think of these as Italian main dishes. Yet while they are important staples on Italy's table, they are most often found as a first course followed by the main, or meat, course. In addition, although pasta and risotto have long been part of the traditional Italian meal, they are not indigenous foods. Wheat originated in Mesopotamia, rice in Asia. Through commerce and the natural course of agricultural trading, these grains found their way to Italy, where they have been interpreted in ways peculiar to the country.*

*Rice was originally imported by the early Romans for medicinal and cosmetic purposes. It was first cultivated in Europe for consumption in the eighth century, planted on the Iberian Peninsula. The* migration to Italy was natural. A thirteenth-century document, a prescription from a hospital near Lucedio, the present estate of Contessa Rosetta Clara Cavalli d'Olivola, substantiates the presence of rice in Piedmont.

Today Italy grows 60 percent of all the rice produced in Europe, providing a high-quality supply. New rulings by the World Trade Organization and the growth of the European Union (EU) are threatening this position, as well as endangering the level of quality. Tons of rice from other members of the EU is now allowed to be exported duty free. The agreement also extends to Africa, the Caribbean, and the Pacific. Unfortunately, this allows rice to be brought in through a European port of transit and repackaged as a European product, allowing importers to avoid duties.

Activists like Contessa Cavalli d'Olivola are building a resistance movement against big industry's efforts to place emphasis on price over quality. "The truth is we shouldn't be selling rice," she says. "We should be exporting the culture of risotto."

Pasta has an even longer history in Italy. It has been traced as far back as the fourth century B.C., as evidenced by pictographs on an Etruscan tomb. Farro, an early forerunner of today's wheat, was probably used to make the pasta. It was high in protein and nutrition, but the yield was low. Eventually, farmers began to crossbreed to create varieties that could meet the demand of the world market. We are beginning to see a comeback of this tasty grain, including its use in pasta.

Due to its worldwide popularity (last year Americans alone bought 1.3 billion pounds), pasta has become a giant business. Highly technologized plants generate an industrial commodity that bears only a visual resemblance to the artisanal pasta of the past. Slick Teflon-coated extrusion machines slide out strands of spaghetti to be flash-dried and packaged. Families like Peduzzi in Abruzzo are fighting to maintain the tradition of old-style pasta. Many of their products are rolled out and shaped by hand, and they use bronze dies to give their extruded pasta the traditional rough texture. Finally, their products are allowed to dry for days before packaging, a practice that maintains the quality and flavor.

Risotto and pasta are such simple foods, yet there is an amazing difference in taste between the industrial products and those treated in traditional ways. At opposite ends of the country, the two artisans profiled here are holding on to methods that will ensure the optimum flavor of their products.

# RICE
## Contessa Rosetta Clara Cavalli d'Olivola
### Principato di Lucedio (Piedmont)

*Driving to visit Contessa Rosetta Clara for the first time was magical. In the middle of the flat plain, the twelfth-century Cistercian abbey rose from the water like a fairy-tale island.*

*Trino, May 1997*

In Vercelli, Piedmont's major rice-growing area, the flat Padano plain rambles from village to village. In May, vast areas are covered with water. Between them, equally vast fields of red poppies burn brightly. Set in the center of this landscape is the Principato di Lucedio, home to the heiress of one of Italy's most renowned rice-producing estates.

Contessa Rosetta Clara Cavalli d'Olivola Salvadori di Wiesenhoff is a descendant of the Marchese di Monferrato, and her family roots sink deep into the soil of the Principato di Lucedio. In 1123, an ancestor, Marchese Ranieri di Monferrato, donated ten thousand hectares (about twenty-five thousand acres) of land to Cistercian monks from La Ferté in Burgundy. An abbey was built on the gift in 1184, and at the same time the monks introduced a crop to the region: rice. They taught the local population new farming methods and ways to increase production, bringing growth to the territory and creating an important economic and cultural center.

When the abbey was secularized in 1784, ownership passed to Vittorio Emanuele, Duke of Aosta, and then to Napoleon. In 1807, Napoleon traded Lucedio to his brother-in-law, the Prince Borghese, in exchange for one-fourth of the art collection in the Galleria Borghese

*Contessa Rosetta Clara Cavalli d'Olivola.*

in Rome. Finally, in 1818, Lucedio was purchased by three investors, one of whom was the Marchese Giovanni Gozani di San Giorgio, a relative of Contessa Rosetta, who became the sole proprietor in 1827.

Lucedio was again sold in 1861 to the Marchese Raffaele de Ferrari, who received the title of Prince of Lucedio as a result of his generous contributions to the Italian state. It remained in his family until 1937, at which time the Contessa's father bought the five-hundred-hectare (over-twelve-hundred-acre) property.

He restored the *secatore*, the area where the rice was allowed to dry in the sun. "Every day the horse would pull the device that would stir the rice, and my father would cover it at night," recalls the Contessa. "It would stay in the sun until December."

Rice grows in many parts of Italy, but thanks to the climate and fresh alpine water, the quality of the grain in Piedmont is superlative. Even though the estate is large, only 10 percent is used for rice cultivation, producing an annual yield of only four thousand pounds. This limited production consists of five types, four of which are sold in the United States. These premium varieties contain two important qualities, high starch for creaminess and hardness that will hold up during cooking and remain al dente. The Arborio variety is the one most commonly known in the United States, undoubtedly because it was the first Italian rice imported on a large scale. Baldo is a variety new to Italy that is low in starch, good for dishes like rice pudding. Carnaroli is the best-quality rice, highest in starch and finest for risotto. The Vialone Nano grain is shorter and thicker, with an indentation on the end. It is excellent for risotto as well, since it holds twice its weight in liquid. And Sant'Andrea, a medium grain with good starch quality, is a type not yet shipped to the United States.

*Unhusked rice.*

Growing rice for risotto is a seven-month process. In April the ground is prepared. All plants, the remains of last year's crop of rice or soybeans, are turned under to enrich the soil. Soybeans are planted as a rotation crop every two to three years, a practice subsidized by the European Union (EU) that allows the farmer to have a cash crop while building up the land. Growing soybeans also helps control invasive weeds. After the old crop is turned under, the tractors break up large pieces of dirt and aerate the fields. Machines with laser eyes precisely flatten the earth, so that when the land is drenched with water it will be evenly flooded.

When everything is ready, the fields are submerged in water from the Canale Cavour, named after the mid-nineteenth-century prime minister who was responsible for building the thousands of water channels. The water is evidence of the health of the area, with an abundance of fish, frogs, and birds, animals that act as natural controls to keep down the insects.

In May the rice is planted. High-quality seed is used to ensure there will be no disease. The water is present until harvest in early fall, although it is occasionally drained and replenished.

In September, at harvest, great mounds of rice are stored inside the buildings of the abbey, kept in the husk to maintain freshness until a purchase order is received. Rice in this condition is called *risone*. "I remember as a child I was allowed to play freely at Lucedio," the Contessa recalls. "I would play in the mountains of rice all the day." When ready to process, the grain is placed in wooden trays and rocked from side to side to separate the chaff. It is then placed in a grinder, where the outer husk is lightly grated, a process that leaves a coating of rice flour, the starch that will later thicken a risotto. This process is done in a nearby *riseria* (rice-processing house), but in the past it was a function of the estate. "After my father died, in 1939, my mother operated a *riseria* here," the Contessa explains. "She was a strong woman, managing fifty workers to grow and clean the rice."

The petite, yet fiery Contessa is the strong woman now. Since 1991, she and her son Paolo have overseen the business, building it into a great success. The first two years they produced only *risone*, but then they began to process and package the finished white rice. Both are politically active in trying to protect the quality of exported rice. The Contessa has earned the title of "Green Contessa," a name that means she is "green with anger." She has been known to climb aboard a tractor and join with the area's farmers to protest government controls on their businesses.

*The land is flooded from May until September, when the rice is harvested.*

The EU regulates not only export quotas, but also the prices of the State Rice Commission. If rice goes unsold on the open market, it can be withdrawn and sold to the commission. At times it is an advantage to the farmer. If harvests are large and the market price is low, the regulated price is more appealing. But, according to new changes in the regulations, the farmer must wait until April, the end of the season, to make that choice. Farmers dependent on the income are finding it difficult to hold out those extra months to reap their rewards. Big industrial operations are not affected like the small family growers are. For that reason, the farmers from Vercelli have formed the Consortium for Rice Sales, which has made an alliance with a local bank to advance money at a low interest rate as early as November. With this new consortium, the farmers also hope to increase the value of high-quality Italian rice.

In the abbey at Lucedio, beneath the frescoed cupola, is a small mountain of Carnaroli rice waiting to be packed into woven cloth bags, packaging that allows it to breathe. The Contessa explains, "Rice is a living thing. If you care for it properly and keep it alive, it will mix well with other ingredients, absorbing the liquid properly; the starch makes it creamy. I don't think you need to add butter at the end, because the flavor of a fresh rice is so good."

# INSALATA DI TONNO E RISO DI ROSETTA CLARA

*Rosetta Clara's Tuna and Rice Salad* - Contessa Rosetta Clara Cavalli d'Olivola

The Contessa's kitchen at her Lucedio estate is surprisingly small. Yet out of this miniscule space she produces delightful meals centered around her rice. She recommends this delicious salad for lunch on a hot day or packed for a picnic.

❧ In a large pot, bring the water to a boil. Add the salt and rice and bring back to a boil, stirring constantly. Reduce the heat to medium and cook, stirring, until the rice is al dente, 15 to 20 minutes.

❧ Pour the rice into a colander and rinse with cold water. When the rice is cool, drain well and spread it on a baking sheet lined with a clean kitchen towel. Let stand for 15 minutes to dry the rice further.

❧ Place the rice in a large bowl, add the olive oil and lemon juice, and toss well. Fold in the tomato, bell pepper, zucchini, celery, tuna, capers, olives, cornichon, Fontina cheese, and basil. Season with salt and pepper.

❧ Transfer the salad to a serving platter and arrange the hard-boiled eggs around the edge. Serve at once.

*SERVES 6 TO 8*

4 quarts water

Salt to taste

1 pound Baldo, Arborio, or Vialone Nano rice

⅔ cup extra-virgin olive oil

¼ cup fresh lemon juice

½ cup seeded and diced ripe tomato

½ cup diced red or green bell pepper

½ cup diced zucchini

½ cup diced celery

1 cup drained tuna packed in olive oil, flaked

2 tablespoons salt-cured capers, rinsed

20 Mediterranean-style oil- or brine-cured black olives, pitted and coarsely chopped

2 tablespoons diced cornichon

¼ pound Val d'Aosta Fontina cheese, diced

¼ cup chopped fresh basil

Freshly ground pepper to taste

4 hard-boiled eggs, peeled and quartered lengthwise

# RISOTTO CON GLI ASPARAGI

*Asparagus Risotto* ~ Contessa Rosetta Clara Cavalli d'Olivola

The Contessa advises to have all the ingredients at room temperature or warmed. If you add a cold ingredient to a cooking risotto, it shocks the rice and slows down the process.

¾ pound asparagus

3 tablespoons unsalted butter

1 tablespoon extra-virgin olive oil

1 tablespoon finely minced scallion

1½ cups Arborio or Carnaroli rice

½ cup dry white wine, at room temperature

1 clove garlic

5 cups chicken stock, heated to a simmer

⅓ cup grated Parmigiano-Reggiano cheese

❧ Cut off the tough root end from each asparagus spear. Peel lightly with a vegetable peeler to within about 2 inches of the tips. Bring a saucepan of salted water to a boil, add the asparagus, and boil until crisp-tender, 3 to 5 minutes; the timing depends on the thickness of the spears. Drain and immediately immerse in ice water to stop the cooking. When cool, drain again and pat dry. Cut into 1-inch pieces. Set aside.

❧ In a heavy 4-quart pot over medium heat, melt the butter with the olive oil. Add the asparagus and scallion and sauté until tender, 4 to 5 minutes. Remove with a slotted spoon and set aside.

❧ Add the rice to the same pot over medium heat. Using a wooden spoon, stir for 1 minute, making sure all the grains are well coated. Add the wine and garlic and stir until the wine is completely absorbed.

❧ Begin to add the simmering stock ½ cup at a time, stirring often to prevent sticking. Wait until the stock is almost completely absorbed before adding the next ½ cup, continually stirring the rice to prevent sticking, and reserving about ¼ cup stock for adding at the end.

❧ After about 18 minutes, when the rice is tender but still firm, add the final ¼ cup stock. Turn off the heat and gently stir in the asparagus and the Parmigiano-Reggiano cheese. Mix well and serve at once.

SERVES 4

# CROQUIS DI RISO

*Rice Croquettes* ~ Contessa Rosetta Clara Cavalli d'Olivola

If the name of this dish sounds French to you, you are right. It is a product of four hundred years of dominance by the House of Savoy in Turin. That royal influence is felt even today in the language, culture, and food. This is a great way to use leftover risotto. Dolcelatte is the milder, sweeter version of Gorgonzola, but any semisoft cheese will be delicious.

& With your hands, form the rice into small oval balls, about 1½ inches in diameter, and tuck a nugget of the cheese into the center of each one. Set the balls aside on a plate as they are formed. You should have 16 balls in all.

& Dip each ball into the egg and then into the bread crumbs, coating well.

& In a skillet, pour in vegetable oil to a depth of 1 inch. Place over medium heat and heat until hot but not smoking. Working in batches so as not to crowd the pan, add the rice balls and fry, turning frequently, until golden brown, 3 to 4 minutes.

& Using a slotted spoon, remove to paper towels to drain briefly. Arrange on a platter and serve at once.

*MAKES 16 CROQUETTES*

*2 cups leftover risotto*

*2 ounces Gorgonzola Dolcelatte cheese, cut into ½-inch nuggets*

*3 eggs, lightly beaten*

*1 cup fine dried bread crumbs, toasted*

*Vegetable oil for frying*

# POMODORI RIPIENI

*Stuffed Tomatoes* ~ Contessa Rosetta Clara Cavalli d'Olivola

The best rice to use in this dish is raw Italian Baldo, but ¼ cup leftover cooked risotto can be used instead. Reduce the cooking time by 10 to 15 minutes if using cooked rice.

12 Roma tomatoes

Salt for tomatoes, plus salt to taste

1 tablespoon raw rice

3 tablespoons minced fresh basil

3 tablespoons tomato paste

2 tablespoons extra-virgin olive oil

2 tablespoons water

❧ Preheat an oven to 300°F. Lightly oil an 8-inch glass baking dish.

❧ Cut a ¼-inch-thick lengthwise slice from one side of each tomato, and set the slices aside. With a small spoon, carefully scoop out the inside of each tomato, leaving walls thick enough for the tomato to maintain its form. Set the pulp aside. Salt the inside of the tomatoes and turn them upside down on a wire rack to drain for 5 minutes.

❧ Pass the tomato pulp through a food mill or sieve placed over a bowl. Add the rice, basil, 1 tablespoon of the tomato paste, and 1 tablespoon of the olive oil. Mix well and season with salt.

❧ Turn the tomatoes hollow side up and fill them with the rice mixture, dividing evenly. Cover with the reserved slices. Place in the prepared baking dish. Drizzle with the remaining 1 tablespoon olive oil. Mix the remaining 2 tablespoons tomato paste with the water and pour around the tomatoes.

❧ Cover the dish and bake until the tomatoes are softened and the rice is tender, 45 to 50 minutes. Serve at once.

*SERVES 6*

# DRY PASTA
## Gianluigi Peduzzi
### Pianella (Abruzzo)

*I don't know why I waited so long to visit Abruzzo. The idea of driving over and through the Gran Sasso mountains was daunting, but ended up being extremely rewarding. The dramatic mountain landscape gave into the turquoise sea surprisingly quickly. And soon we found ourselves in beach chairs on the sand, savoring the warm, moist day.*

*Pescara, June 1998*

The rural landscape of Abruzzo is scattered with medieval walled cities and ancient monasteries. Three hours east of Rome, on the Adriatic Sea, the region rises at once to the peaceful snow-capped southern Apennines, the backbone of Italy. The seaside port of Pescara bustles with commerce and transportation across the Adriatic, but inland the population is sparse and the surroundings serene.

Due to the natural mountain barrier, Abruzzo rides the saddle between the north and south of Italy, but the temperament of the food is distinctly southern. The proximity to the wheat-producing area of Apulia has made this a historic center for pasta, famous for classics such as *maccheroni alla chitarra.* Using a rectangular wooden frame stretched with steel strings like a guitar, the dough is cut into long strands. It is usually served with *profumi,* assorted seasonal vegetables and the intensely aromatic mountain herbs.

In the tiny village of Pianella, Gianluigi Peduzzi oversees Rustichella d'Abruzzo, the pasta-making business started by his great-grandfather, Rafaele Sergiacomo, in the nearby auspiciously named city of Penne. Sergiacomo stone- ground his flour from local durum wheat and *farro* with a water-powered mill, and

*Gianluigi Peduzzi.*

was the first pasta manufacturer to have a mill driven by electricity.

*Farro (Triticum dicoccum),* an ancient wheat strain, is still grown locally, and the Rustichella *farro* pastas are made with 100 percent of the grain. The rest of the dried pastas are made with 85 percent semolina (hard durum wheat from Apulia) and 15 percent hard Canadian wheat. The flour is always milled twenty-four hours or less before using it to make dough. "We sell a lot of fresh pasta here in Italy," says Gianluigi. "We use whole-wheat flour for that and approximately two thousand eggs a day. Most of the egg pasta you buy has only four eggs for each kilo [a little over two pounds] of flour. We use seven eggs."

All of the extruded pastas are made with bronze dies created by Gianluigi's grandfather Gaetano in the thirties. This coarse metal surface gives the pasta a roughened texture that helps it hold the sauce. "I lived with my grandfather for six years when I was in high school and worked with him," Gianluigi recalls. "Monday through Friday he made the pasta, and on Saturday he sold it at the market. In July and August he traded fresh pasta for grain. He knew about semolina just by holding it in his hand: if it stuck to his palm, it was fresh; otherwise it was too dry."

    After extrusion or shaping, the pasta is flash-dried in an oven for a few minutes, then "left to breathe," air-dried, for fifty-six hours in temperature-controlled chambers. This process differs greatly from industrial pasta, which is dried at high temperatures for eight to fifteen hours, at the most, and then packaged. "High-heat drying kills the pasta, kills the flavor," Gianluigi explains. "It takes me one year to make what big industry makes in one day."

    In 1981, Gianluigi and his father, Piero, assumed the business and focused on a higher-end market. Packaging changed, reverting back to grandfather Rafaele's simple brown-bag wrapper. The product was the same, a classic high-quality pasta. Today, Rustichella creates over 110 varieties, a diversity designed to meet the individual markets of each region. Thirty of those are exported to the United States, including the classic spaghetti, rigatoni, and linguine made simply with semolina of durum wheat and water, as well as the familiar *fusilli col buco*, a long, wavy, hollow corkscrew strand. Assorted egg pastas, including wide, flat *pappardelle* and fettuccine flavored with locally grown saffron, are made with eggs from free-range chickens. There are several unique shapes, such as the irregular diamond-shaped *taccozzette*, "little wood chips," and especially the handmade forms: the tricolored, curly-surfaced *spugnole* made with spinach and tomato; *orecchiette,* "little ears"; twisted *strozzapreti*, or "priest stranglers"; and *pasta al ceppo*, literally "pasta on a stick," made by wrapping the dough around tiny sticks. In addition, Gianluigi has revived traditional Abruzzese pasta shapes, such as *strozzacavalli* (horse stranglers) and the cone-like *torchietti.* These hearty pastas are especially good for baked pasta dishes like the *timballo di maccheroni* on page 54.

    The difference in ingredients and method is demonstrated in the taste. Most dried pastas rely on the sauce to make them shine, but these pastas are delicious with just a little olive oil and grated Parmigiano-Reggiano cheese. Fresh-milled flour and water from pure mountain springs start the product, but time and the gentle touch of Gianluigi and his family develop it into a premium commodity. The company motto sums it up: *Acqua, Vento, Aria, Terra, Uomo: sono gli ingrediente alla base di tutte la specialità Rustichella d'Abruzzo*, "Water, Wind, Air, Earth, Man: these are the main ingredients of the specialties of Rustichella d'Abruzzo."

*Gianluigi Peduzzi's mother, Nicolina.*

# RIGATONCINI CON TONNO, LIMONE, CAPPERI, E OLIVE

*Rigatoncini with Tuna, Lemon, Capers, and Olives* ~ Rolando Beramendi

Rolando Beramendi has been seeking out and importing Italy's best products since 1987. His company, Manicaretti Imports, has one of the best reputations with professional chefs and home cooks alike, specializing in products from family estates and artisanal producers, including Rustichella pasta (see Resources, page 163). Fresh seafood and this ridged tube pasta are a natural marriage, especially when joined with the south's abundant lemons, capers, and olives.

*1 pound* rigatoncini, *or other short tube pasta*

*½ cup extra-virgin olive oil*

*1 lemon, quartered and thinly sliced*

*4 cloves garlic, minced*

*24 Mediterranean-style oil-cured black olives, pitted and roughly chopped*

*2 tablespoons salt-cured capers, rinsed*

*1 pound tuna fillet, cut into 1-inch cubes*

*Sea salt and freshly ground pepper to taste*

*¼ cup minced fresh flat-leaf parsley*

❧ Bring a large saucepan of salted water to a boil. Add the pasta, stir well, and cook until al dente, about 10 minutes.

❧ While the pasta is cooking, in a skillet over medium heat, warm the olive oil. Add the lemon slices and sauté gently until softened, about 2 minutes. Add the garlic and sauté for another minute. Stir in the olives and capers. Then add the tuna and sauté until firm to the touch, about 3 minutes. Season with salt and pepper.

❧ Drain the pasta and and transfer it to a large serving bowl. Top with the tuna and sauce and garnish with the parsley. Serve at once.

*SERVES 4 TO 6*

# SIAMESI AL FARRO ALL'ABRUZZESE
*Farro Pasta with Tomato, Olives, and Basil* ~ Gianluigi Peduzzi

High in protein, flour milled from *farro* makes a dense and delicious pasta that is typically prepared in the countryside with fresh seasonal vegetables. The *siamesi* shape, literally "Siamese," is two strands of pasta twisted together. If you have difficulty finding *farro* pasta, substitute a whole-wheat pasta.

❧ Bring a large saucepan of salted water to a boil. Add the pasta, stir well, and cook until al dente, about 10 minutes.

❧ While the pasta is cooking, in a large bowl, combine the tomato, olives, garlic, basil, and pepper flakes. Add the olive oil and toss well. Season with salt and pepper.

❧ Drain the pasta and add to the bowl. Toss well and add the Parmigiano-Reggiano cheese. Mix well and serve at once.

*SERVES 4*

½ pound farro siamesi *pasta*

1 ripe tomato, peeled, seeded, and diced

¼ cup pitted and roughly chopped Mediterranean-style oil-cured black olives

1 clove garlic, minced

5 or 6 small fresh basil leaves

Pinch of chile pepper flakes

½ cup extra-virgin olive oil

Salt and freshly ground pepper to taste

Grated Parmigiano-Reggiano cheese to taste

# CONCHIGLIONI DI SPINACI E RICOTTA CON SALSA DI ASPARGI

*Shells Stuffed with Spinach and Ricotta in Asparagus Sauce* - Gianluigi Peduzzi

This is a wonderful do-ahead dish made by Gianluigi's mother, Nicolina. Completely assemble the stuffed large shells and sauce and refrigerate until ready to heat and serve. In spring, asparagus is a fresh and colorful addition to the sauce. In other seasons, try broccoli, carrots, or squash.

& Bring a large saucepan of salted water to a boil. Add the pasta shells, stir gently, and cook until al dente, about 8 minutes. Drain and set aside to cool.

& To make the sauce, in a large skillet over medium-high heat, warm the olive oil. Add the onion, carrot, and celery and sauté until lightly browned, 5 to 7 minutes. Add the tomatoes and parsley, reduce the heat to low, cover, and cook until slightly thickened, about 30 minutes. Add the asparagus tips and set aside.

& In a small saucepan over low heat, melt the butter, then whisk in the flour. Cook, stirring, over low heat for 3 to 4 minutes to cook away the raw taste of the flour. Do not allow to brown. Add the milk, while stirring constantly, raise the heat to medium, and continue to cook, stirring occasionally, until slightly thickened, 3 to 5 minutes. Stir into the tomato sauce, season with salt and pepper, and set aside.

& To make the filling, in a bowl, combine the ricotta, spinach, and the egg. Season with nutmeg, salt, and pepper; set aside.

& Preheat an oven to 375°F. Lightly butter two 9-by-13-inch flameproof baking pans.

& Spoon the ricotta mixture into the pasta shells and place them in the prepared pans. Add the sauce over and around the filled shells. Bake until completely warmed through, 15 to 20 minutes. Remove from the oven and sprinkle with the Parmigiano-Reggiano cheese.

& Turn the oven to broil and slip the pans under the broiler. Broil until golden brown, 3 to 4 minutes. Serve at once.

*SERVES 6*

1 pound conchiglioni *(large pasta shells)*

**For the sauce:**

*3 tablespoons extra-virgin olive oil*

*1 onion, diced*

*1 carrot, peeled and diced*

*1 celery stalk, diced*

*2 pounds ripe tomatoes, peeled and coarsely chopped*

*1 tablespoon minced fresh flat-leaf parsley*

*Tips only from 1 pound asparagus, parboiled until crisp-tender*

*2 tablespoons unsalted butter*

*2 tablespoons unbleached all-purpose flour*

*1 cup milk*

*Salt and freshly ground pepper to taste*

**For the filling:**

*21 ounces (scant 3 cups) ricotta cheese*

*1 pound spinach, steamed, squeezed dry, and chopped*

*1 egg, lightly beaten*

*Freshly grated nutmeg to taste*

*Salt and freshly ground pepper to taste*

*½ cup grated Parmigiano-Reggiano cheese*

# ORECCHIETTE ALL'ABRUZZESE

*Orecchiette with Clams and Broccoli Rabe* - Gianluigi Peduzzi

This dish is a favorite in Pescara, a major fishing port on the Adriatic. The *orecchiette*, little ear-shaped shells like tiny flat cups, hold the delicious sauce in their recesses. The Abruzzese like this dish spicy, but you can adjust the seasoning to your taste.

*3 dozen clams, scrubbed*

*1 cup dry white wine*

*1 pound dried orecchiette*

*3 tablespoons extra-virgin olive oil*

*4 cloves garlic, minced*

*½ cup chopped onion*

*½ pound broccoli rabe, tough stems removed and cut into ½-inch pieces*

*3 ripe tomatoes, peeled, seeded, and coarsely chopped*

*1 tablespoon fresh flat-leaf parsley, minced*

*Pinch of chile pepper flakes*

*Salt and freshly ground pepper to taste*

Place the clams in a large pot, discarding any that do not close to the touch. Add the wine, cover, and cook over high heat for 1 minute. Uncover and remove clams that have opened, placing them in a bowl. Re-cover and continue to cook the remaining clams over high heat for a few seconds longer, or until they open. Discard any clams that fail to open. When cooled enough to handle, remove the clam meats from their shells, discarding the shells and taking care to capture any juices. Chop the meats coarsely and set aside. Strain the cooking liquid and juices through a fine-mesh sieve (preferably lined with cheesecloth). Set aside.

Bring a large saucepan of salted water to a boil. Add the pasta, stir well, and cook until al dente, 8 to 10 minutes.

While the pasta is cooking, in a large skillet over medium heat, warm the olive oil. Add the garlic and onion and sauté until softened, but not browned, 2 to 3 minutes. Add the broccoli rabe and cook, stirring often, until barely tender, 5 to 7 minutes. Add the tomatoes, clams, and reserved cooking liquid and heat through.

Drain the pasta and add it to the skillet holding the clam mixture. Toss well and stir in the parsley, pepper flakes, salt, and pepper.

Transfer to a serving bowl and serve at once.

*SERVES 6*

# FRESH PASTA
## Laura Galli, *Hosteria Giusti*
### Modena (Emilia-Romagna)

Laura Galli and her husband, Nano Morandi, are the dynamic force at Modena's Hosteria Giusti, a four-table dining room behind the four-hundred-year-old Salumeria Giusti. Laura's cooking is renowned —a table is available by advance reservation only— especially her delicate handmade *stracchetti*, *gargonelli*, *tortelloni*, *tagliolini*, and *tagliatelle*. Fresh pasta in Emilia-Romagna is rich in eggs. For each batch, Laura uses about five eggs for every pound of flour. She never uses oil in her pasta dough because it makes it too slippery to hold the sauce.

Many pasta makers use a marble surface to work on, but Laura mounds her flour on a large wooden table. She cracks the eggs into a well in the center of the mound and gradually works them into the flour with her fingertips, incorporating the flour a little at a time. Her arms are strong from the daily vigorous kneading required to make the dough smooth.

Laura's rolling pin is four feet long, the width of her worktable. With it, she rolls out the dough into a thin sheet. After letting it dry for approximately a quarter of an hour, she cuts it into the desired shape.

*Laura Galli at work.*

# VII

## *SWEET ENDINGS*

### CHOCOLATE
Roberto Catinari
Giorgio Marangoni

### DOLCI
Anna Scolastica Altavilla

### *VIN SANTO DI TOSCANA*
Ettore Falvo, *wine maker*

*Biscotti di Prato*

### HONEY
Guido Franci

# VII

# SWEET ENDINGS

The best desserts I've had in Italy were the simplest: *a slice of pear with some pecorino cheese, warm ricotta drizzled with chestnut honey, tiny wild strawberries sprinkled with* aceto balsamico tradizionale. *In pastry shops from the far north to Sicily, there are elaborate concoctions of pastry cream and nougat and nuts and honey.*

*Chocolate was introduced to Europe in 1528, when the Spanish brought it back from the Americas. Italians have their own chocolate history. Some say it was chocolate's second stop in Europe, after Spain. By the 1600s, Turin was a major center for chocolate, which was still primarily consumed in the form of a drink. Some sources say that it was the Italians who introduced it to Switzerland. In any case, it wasn't until 1875 that a Swiss man, Daniel Peter, began blending it with milk to create the milk chocolate we love today. This led to the Italian blend of chocolate with hazelnuts to make the divine* gianduia *and a great many other variations. Some of the oldest chocolate-making families in Italy have become major commercial producers, such as Peyrano, Perugina, and Majani. But a few artisans remain, hand-dipping chocolates and filling them with special treats.*

*After chocolate, baked goods are the most popular sweet snacks, enjoyed with an espresso, after dinner, and even for breakfast. Every region has its own special cookie. Biscotti, twice-baked cookies, are the most famous by American standards, but a wealth of other bite-sized delights exist.*

*It would take another whole book to talk about the Italian wine artisans. Since food is my specialty, I've left that to the wine writers. But I couldn't resist including just one. I am among the lucky few have tasted the magnificent* vin santo *made by Avignonesi in Montepulciano. This wine is but one component of the Falvo family's approach to quality, which they call* classica. *It begins with their treatment of wines, of course, but then reaches into every aspect of their lives. For example, Alberto Falvo is bringing back the Murgese horse, the last of the true Italian breeds. And wine maker Ettore Falvo is breeding the native Cinta Senese pig, which produces a fine prosciutto. They also seek out artisans such as a master blacksmith specializing in ancient mechanisms to design the perfect rotisserie. Thus, it comes as no surprise that their wines are first-rate.*

# CHOCOLATE
## Roberto Catinari, Agliana (Tuscany)
## Giorgio Marangoni, Macerata (Marches)

*We had just finished the meal at Badia a Coltibuono when the waiter brought a little plate of chocolates. I took a dainty bite from the first one before he could warn me. At once, a sweet liquid ran down my chin. I followed instructions for the next one, to pop the whole thing in my mouth, or else. Grappa! Inside a chocolate!*

*Chianti, May 1992*

### Roberto Catinari, Agliana (Tuscany)

In the tiny village of Agliana, about thirty minutes from Florence, is a sweet little chocolate shop. Upstairs, Roberto Catinari applies his twenty years of experience in Switzerland to his twenty-five years of Italian interpretation. The result is a first-class product sold in coffee bars and pastry shops in Naples, Rome, and Milan. The chocolates I tasted at Badia a Coltibuono were his, procured by his brother, who was the chef there at the time.

These liqueur-filled delights are Catinari's signature chocolate. To make them, he creates a mold in the desired shape. First he fills a box with sifted cornstarch and carefully smooths the surface. Then the impression is made in the cornstarch with the desired shape and filled with a liquid composed of sugar syrup and the liqueur of choice. My favorite is a chocolate in the shape of a champagne cork filled with champagne! Another thin layer of cornstarch is sifted over the top and the form is left to harden for a day. As the liquid sets up, the sugar crystallizes against the starch, making a chrysalis-fragile container that will hold the liqueur. These shapes are then dipped by hand in chocolate. Catinari also uses grappa, *vin santo*, and fruit liqueurs to fill the molds.

*Roberto Catinari.*

The shapes and flavors change with the seasons. For example, in the fall Catinari hand-shapes chestnuts from *gianduia*. A tiny hook, screwed into the end, is held as three-fourths of the "chestnut" is dipped into chocolate and then hung on a wire line to dry. The weight of the chocolate dripping off the bottom forms a small point. The end result looks remarkably like a real chestnut.

The chocolatier's art is demonstrated in Catinari's "antique" chocolate tools. A large, shallow box is filled with finely sifted cocoa powder. He carefully makes an impression in the cocoa with an antique tool, such as a pair of pliers or an old skeleton key. Gently, he lifts the metal tool away to reveal a duplicate shape pressed in the cocoa. With skill and patience, he fills the impression with melted chocolate, ensuring that every little nook and crevice is filled. The surface is finished with a dusting of cocoa, and the chocolate is left to harden. The same process is used for "candleholders," except that it is repeated for the reverse side of the shape. After the chocolate has set, the two halves are joined and dusted with more cocoa to finish the antique look.

## Giorgio Marangoni, Macerata (Marches)

The two Marangoni brothers, Giorgio and Alfredo, and their sister, Lorian, come from a long line of pastry makers. Their great-great-grandfather started a bakery in Macerata in the mid-1800s, which later, in the 1950s, became a pastry shop.

The evolution has continued, with this generation taking up artisanal chocolate making. Giorgio, the eldest brother, studied with Belgian chocolate makers working in Italy and brought the secrets back to Macerata. All of the work is done by hand or with simple machines. Traditional recipes play an important role, but the family has made many innovations.

One specialty is chocolate-covered dried figs. First the fig is soaked in rum. Once softened, it is stuffed with walnut pieces and carefully hand-dipped in chocolate. The finished morsel is wrapped individually with paper and twine.

Other seasonal fresh fruits are covered with chocolate as well, including gooseberries, raisins, blueberries, plums, chestnuts, and cherries, to name a few. The family has also long been experimenting with combining aromatic flavors with chocolate. "The mimosa flower has a remarkable scent," says Giorgio, "but when you try to work with it, the wonderful

*Marangoni fills chocolates with herb-infused honey.*

fragrance disappears, and you are left with a *puzzo*, a bad smell." There have been many successes, though, such as chocolates filled with honey that has been infused with herbs and spices. Some of the unusual combinations include honey flavored with a mixture of fresh herbs such as basil, sage, mint, rosemary, and fennel flower. Giorgio warms the Sicilian orange-flower honey in a bain-marie and adds the herbs. After approximately four months, the honey is ready to use, fragrant with each herb's unique scent. Some spices— nutmeg, cinnamon, ginger, even saffron—are also used to infuse the honey. When paired with chocolate, the result is a pleasant surprise. The chocolate coats your mouth and remains as you taste the flavored honey. It is a completely new taste sensation.

I asked Giorgio if he knew anything about the mythical "jasmine chocolate" known in the court of the Cosimo I, the Grand Duke of Tuscany. "No," he replied, "but maybe we could try and make that. . . ."

*Lorian, Alfredo, and Giorgio Marangoni.*

# DOLCI
## Anna Scolastica Altavilla
### Norcia (Umbria)

*I've fallen in love with Umbria, a place of great contrasts. After three serene nights on a tiny island in the middle of Lago Trasimeno, I wound over spectacular mountain roads to the other side of the region and arrived in Norcia. I came here seeking black truffles and found, in addition, a precious jewel of a town.*

*Norcia, November 1993*

Umbria, known as the "green heart of Italy," is a landscape of hilltop towns and tiny picturesque villages perched on the sides of green valleys. Even though it is Italy's only landlocked region, it is not lacking in water: the terrain is ribboned by trout-filled streams and rivers and dotted with lakes, including Trasimeno, one of the largest in the country.

This diverse region is known also for its wealth of black truffles. Norcia, tucked into the crevices of the oak-lined Sibillini Mountains, enjoys a rich fall and winter season that culminates in a late-winter truffle festival. The oaks also provide plentiful acorns that are fed to the local pigs. Norcia's fame for processed pork products has led pork butchers all over Italy to call themselves *norcini.*

And if the truffles and pigs were not enough claim to fame, Norcia was also the home of Saint Benedict, the founder of monasticism, and Scolastica, his twin sister. I mention this fact because Scolastica is the name of a wonderful pastry cook whose shop stands on the main street of Norcia.

"All of the little children call me *la dolce cocchina,*" says the plump and smiling Anna Scolastica Altavilla. Since 1979, her pastry case has been full of baked treasures of many shapes and sizes. The nearby mountains yield such baking ingredients as chestnuts, pine nuts, hazelnuts, honey, almonds,

*Anna Scolastica Altavilla.*

cherries, and wild berries. Anna fills her pastries with all of these.

Never married, Anna spends most of her time baking, single-handedly running the *pasticceria.* She pulls out a photocopy of an entry in Fred Plotkin's *Italy for the Gourmet Traveler.* "Why do you want to write about me?" she asks. "I'm not sure I need any more business."

Anna's kitchen is small and full of the clutter of twenty years: photos and recipes tacked on the walls, pots and strainers hanging from hooks, and pastry scrapers and spatulas tucked into handy spaces. She works with a knowledge of her ingredients. *Pasta frolla* is the basis of many of her pastries, a short pastry crust rich in butter and livened with the zest of lemon. "You need to make it quickly so that your hands don't warm the butter," she says, as she deftly blends the butter into the flour. "Sometimes I use a portion of *farro* flour in the pastry. It's heavier, but it has a good flavor."

Anna's repertoire is extensive and includes regional classics such as *serpentone,* a pastry filled with almonds, raisins, candied fruit, and aniseed and shaped like a big snake with raisin eyes, and *ciambelline,* a sweet ring of bread she makes with *vin santo.* "Have you had a *cioccolatini di Norcia?*" she asks, as she hands me one. "It is melted chocolate—I only use Perugina—chopped hazelnuts, and popped *farro.*"

# PASTA FROLLA

*Pastry Dough* ~ Anna Scolastica Altavilla

Anna uses this basic short pastry with most of her baked goods. She adds a little bicarbonate for a flakier dough that will handle her moist fillings. A blend of baking powder and baking soda will yield a similar effect.

    &#x2767; In a large bowl, combine the flour, sugar, salt, baking powder, and baking soda. Using your fingertips, work the butter pieces into the flour mixture, blending to form crumbly pea-sized pieces.

    &#x2767; In another bowl, combine the eggs, lemon zest, and vanilla. Mix well. With a fork, stir the eggs into the flour mixture, blending just until incorporated. Transfer to a lightly floured work surface and press the dough gently into a smooth disk about 10 inches in diameter. Wrap in plastic and chill for at least 1 hour.

*MAKES 1 DOUBLE OR 2 SINGLE 10-INCH CRUSTS*

4¾ cups unbleached all-purpose flour

2 cups sugar

Pinch of salt

½ teaspoon baking powder

½ teaspoon baking soda

1 pound chilled unsalted butter,
    cut into small pieces

5 eggs

Grated zest of 1 lemon

½ teaspoon vanilla extract

# RAVIOLINI DI RICOTTA

*Sweet Ricotta Ravioli* ~ Anna Scolastica Altavilla

"The ricotta is good here, from the mountains," says Anna. She likes to flavor the ricotta in these sweet pastries with a variety of flavors, replacing the cocoa with rum or anise or just tucking a little piece of Perugina chocolate inside.

*1 recipe* Pasta Frolla *(page 156)*

*8 ounces (about 1 cup) ricotta cheese*

*½ cup sugar, plus sugar for dusting*

*1 egg yolk, plus 1 whole egg*

*1 tablespoon grated orange zest*

*2 tablespoons cocoa powder*

*Sugar*

❧ Preheat an oven to 375°F. Line a baking sheet with parchment paper.

❧ To make the filling, in a bowl combine the ricotta, the ½ cup sugar, egg yolk, and orange zest. Mix well. Sift in the cocoa powder and stir to blend well. Set aside.

❧ On a lightly floured work surface, roll out the dough ¼ inch thick. Using a 3-inch biscuit cutter, cut out 24 rounds.

❧ Working on a lightly floured work surface, spoon 1 tablespoon of the ricotta filling onto half of each round. Fold in half and pinch the edges to seal. Place on the prepared baking sheet. Beat the whole egg lightly, and brush over the tops of the pastries. Dust generously with sugar.

❧ Bake until golden brown, 20 to 25 minutes. Remove to a wire rack to cool completely. Serve warm or at room temperature.

*MAKES 2 DOZEN PASTRIES*

# PAN DI SPAGNA
*Sponge Cake* ~ Anna Scolastica Altavilla

This recipe arrived in Italy with the Spanish conquerors, hence its name. It is a versatile sponge cake that is often used for layering with cream fillings and fresh fruits. Anna also uses it in the bottom of her tartlets, to absorb the excess juices from the cooking fruit.

❧ Preheat an oven to 350°F. Line a baking sheet with parchment paper. Lightly butter the parchment and the sides of the pan.

❧ In a bowl, using an electric mixer, beat together the egg yolks and vanilla. Add ½ cup of the sugar and beat until light and creamy.

❧ In another bowl, using clean beaters, whip the egg whites and salt until frothy. Gradually add the remaining ¼ cup sugar, whipping constantly until soft peaks form.

❧ Gently fold the egg whites into the egg yolks. Fold in the flour mixture in three additions, taking care not to overmix the batter. Pour into the prepared pan and smooth the surface.

❧ Bake until the top is firm, but not browned, 20 to 25 minutes. Remove to a wire rack, loosen the edges with a knife, and invert the cake onto the rack. Let cool slightly before removing the parchment paper.

*MAKES 1 SHEET CAKE*

*3 eggs, separated*

*½ teaspoon vanilla extract*

*¾ cup sugar*

*Pinch of salt*

*½ cup unbleached all-purpose flour, sifted with ¼ teaspoon baking powder*

# CESTINI DI MELE

*Apple Baskets* - Anna Scolastica Altavilla

Anna uses seasonal fruits for these little mouthfuls. In the summer she uses blackberries and in the spring fresh cherries. When these fruits are abundant, she makes preserves to bake with in the colder seasons.

*1 recipe* Pasta Frolla *(page 156)*

*6 tart apples such as Pippin or Granny Smith, peeled, cored, and diced*

*½ cup sugar*

*½ cup raisins*

*3 tablespoons rum*

*1 recipe* Pan di Spagna *(page 158)*

❧ Preheat an oven to 375°F. Lightly butter twenty-four 3-inch tartlet pans.

❧ On a lightly floured work surface, roll out the dough ¼ inch thick. Using a 3-inch biscuit cutter, cut out 24 rounds. Gently press the rounds into the tartlet pans. Trim the edges even with the rims. Place the tartlet pans on a baking sheet and chill until the dough is firm, about 30 minutes.

❧ In a bowl, combine the apples, sugar, raisins, and rum. Toss well and set aside.

❧ Cut the *Pan di Spagna* into twenty-four 1-inch squares. Place a square on the bottom of each tartlet. Arrange the apple filling over each cake layer, generously filling the pans.

❧ Bake until the edge of each tartlet crust is golden brown and the apples are slightly tender, about 20 minutes. Serve warm or at room temperature.

*MAKES 2 DOZEN TARTLETS*

# VIN SANTO DI TOSCANA
## Ettore Falvo, wine maker
### Montepulciano (Tuscany)

In the early fourteenth century, the Pope resided for a time in southern France, in Avignon. When he returned to Rome in 1377, he was joined by some of the noble families of Avignon. These came to be known as the Avignonesi, and their legacy has endured. The Palazzo Avignonesi in Montepulciano, built in the late 1500s, rests on top of an Etruscan dome that can be viewed from the wine cellars. Today, the winery produces world-class wines under Ettore Falvo, who married the last of the Avignonesi family line in the early seventies and merged their properties to found the company Avignonesi. "Our philosophy is that acquired wisdom, years of experience, and taste are refined by time," explains Ettore.

Time is one of the essential elements in Avignonesi's highly acclaimed *Vin santo di Toscana*. The company produces two very particular types of *vin santo*. The first, *Vin santo di Toscana*, is made with three traditional Italian white grapes, Grechetto, Malvasia Toscana, and Trebbiano Toscano. The rarified Occhio di Pernice, "Eye of the Partridge," is made using one-third red Prugnolo Gentile grapes.

In late September, the grapes are hand-selected from La Selva, a southern Tuscan vineyard on the hills of the Chiuso di Cortona. Carefully chosen for sweetness, they must be in perfectly formed clusters that are free of blemishes to prevent them from molding as they age on the drying mats.

The *vinsantaia* is the warm and dry, well-ventilated room where the grapes are left to raisin. It is actually comprised of two chambers. The *appassitoio* is the room where the grapes are dried, and the *vinsantaia*

*Ettore Falvo.*

proper is the aging room. Each room is about 220 square feet, with symmetrical windows that ensure a continuous flow of air. The roof is not insulated and the windows are always kept open. The freshly picked grapes are laid upon *cannicci*, mats made by a local artisan from reeds that grow in the nearby lakes. The uneven texture of their surface allows the air to flow between the grapes to dry the bunches evenly. When the grapes have reached the proper balance of sugar and acidity, they are crushed. "After about six months, I check them visually, and by tasting them," Ettore explains. "When I think they are ready, I do an analysis to make sure that I have 60 percent sugar and 0.6 percent acidity."

Crushing takes place in the beginning of April. The thick must is then clarified by decantation and refrigeration and placed in fifty-liter *caratelli*, Slavonian oak barrels. The barrels are sealed at once with a linen cloth, a cork, and red sealing wax and left to age undisturbed for eight years. These barrels, which are twenty to thirty years old, are never completely emptied, for the magic of the Avignonesi *vin santo* comes from the *madre,* the "mother." It is a thick, dark, concentrated mixture of lees from previous vintages, and it provides the inoculation to begin fermentation. Ettore says, "The mother in our *vin santo* goes back to the year 1500, or perhaps earlier, since the time when *vin santo* was first made."

Because the barrels are exposed to the climate in the uninsulated aging room, the first fermentation in spring is slow. It speeds up with the summer heat, only to slow down again in the next season. This cycle is repeated through each season of aging. Most *vin santo* is aged for a minimum of three years, but Ettore Falvo leaves it to mature for eight. "Fermentation is very slow, and needs a period of at least three years to complete. During the first year, the liquid reaches about 2 percent alcohol, which is increased by another 6 to 7 percent during the second, and so on, until it peaks at around 16 percent, the maximum level tolerable by the yeasts. The yeasts are therefore self-containing. Any further aging increases the concentration of the *vin santo* by augmenting both flavor and taste. We leave the Occhio di Pernice to age for ten years."

The *vin santo* is removed by inserting a small tube that cannot reach the bottom of the barrel. The liquid is sucked out, leaving the *madre* in place at the depths of the cask. Then the mother is poured into another container. Newly pressed must is introduced to the barrels, which are never washed, and the mother is redistributed among them.

The finished *vin santo* is bottled and aged six months longer to let it recover from the stressful process of bottling. The end result is a thick, aureate nectar with a bouquet that is intense, full-bodied, persistent, and complex, reminiscent of dried fruits, spices, and vanilla. The concentration yields 16.5 percent alcohol.

The name *vin santo* is attributed to a remark by Cardinal Bessarione in 1440, who, upon tasting the wine, reportedly exclaimed, *"Ma questo è un vino santo!"*—"But, this is a holy wine!" In fact, for hundreds of years it was used by Catholic priests for Mass.

*Vin santo* is often designated as a dessert wine and is commonly served with *biscotti.* The Avignonesi version is more appropriately called a meditative wine. Only three thousand bottles (0.375 liter each) of *Vin santo di Toscana* are released each year, and only one thousand Occhio di Pernice. It is a rare and divine potion. No sane person would dip a cookie into this elixir. Ettore recommends to sip it slowly from a large, wide glass to enhance—and appreciate—the aroma.

# BISCOTTI DI PRATO
## *Almond Biscotti*

Americans equate the name *biscotti* with the crispy cookies famous for dipping in *vin santo*. In Italy, however, *biscotti* can mean any number of little cookies. The name literally means "cooked again," and describes the method of first baking a cakelike log, then slicing it and baking again.

*Biscotti di Prato,* from a medieval city near Florence, is certainly one of the more recognized versions. Also called *cantucci,* they are delicious with coffee. In Prato, the *biscotti* are made with bitter almonds, but domestic unblanched almonds will substitute well. The skin imparts a slightly bitter taste reminiscent of the true flavor.

*1 cup whole unblanched almonds*
*1¾ cups cake flour*
*1 cup unbleached all-purpose flour*
*1 teaspoon salt*
*1 teaspoon baking powder*
*½ teaspoon baking soda*
*4 eggs*
*¾ cup sugar*
*2 teaspoons vanilla extract*
*1 tablespoon grated orange zest*

❧ Preheat an oven to 325°F. Spread the almonds on a baking sheet and bake until golden brown, 12 to 15 minutes. Transfer to a cool surface and let cool completely.

❧ Line the baking sheet with parchment paper. In a large bowl, combine the cake flour, all-purpose flour, salt, baking powder, baking soda, and the cooled almonds. Mix well.

❧ In another bowl, beat together the eggs and sugar until light. Add the vanilla and orange zest and mix well. Stir the egg mixture into the dry ingredients, stirring just until blended. Do not overmix. The dough will be sticky. Moisten your fingers with water and transfer the dough to the prepared baking sheet, forming a log about 3 inches wide.

❧ Bake at 325°F until a toothpick inserted into the center comes out clean, about 30 minutes. Remove the log to a wire rack to cool. Reduce the oven temperature to 275°F. Replace the parchment paper on the baking sheet.

❧ Cut the log on the diagonal into 1/2-inch-thick slices. Place them on the lined baking pan. Bake until the cookies are a pale golden brown, about 20 minutes. Remove to wire racks to cool.

*MAKES 2 DOZEN COOKIES*

# HONEY
## Guido Franci
### Montalcino (Tuscany)

*Fresh, fresh ricotta, still warm from its cooking, drizzled with smoky chestnut honey. Sublime.*

*Lucca, June 1987*

At eighty-eight, Guido Franci has made his mark in the honey world. For sixty-four years his vocation has been bees. "I was twenty-five when I started," says Guido. "I love working with bees because they are diligent laborers and they make a very sweet thing, the honey."

Now, with the help of his nephew and his wife, Dina, he manages seven to eight hundred hives. "I used to have more, but it is a hard work. We move the little houses and the families of bees from place to place, to follow the flowers in bloom."

Honey is heavily influenced by regional and seasonal changes in vegetation. The flavor of chestnut flower honey is rich and smoky, while the honey of alpine flowers is delicate. In the south of Italy, there is a bitter honey, made from the *corbezzolo* bush, also known as arbutus.

"Bees are important to man," says Guido. "They help keep the environment in balance, and pollinate the flowers so that we have a beautifully colored landscape."

*Guido Franci has been bottling honey for sixty-four years.*

# RESOURCES

**Culinary Guides to Italy**
Slow Food
Via Mendicità Istruita, 14
12042 Bra (CN), Italy
Tel. (01139) 0172.41.12.73; Fax (01139) 0172.42.12.93.
*An organization devoted to the fight against fast food. It publishes excellent guides to the gastronomic pleasures of Italy.*

Capalbo, Carla. *The Food Lover's Companion to Tuscany.* San Francisco: Chronicle Books, 1998.

Millon, Marc, and Kim Millon. *The Food Lover's Companion to Italy.* New York: Little, Brown, 1996.

Plotkin, Fred. *Italy for the Gourmet Traveler.* New York: Little, Brown, 1996.

Willinger, Faith Heller. *Eating in Italy.* New York: Morrow, 1996.

**Culinary Excursions to Italy**
Week-long excursions in Tuscany, Emilia-Romagna, and Piedmont
Culinary Arts, Intl.
1324 State Street, J-157
Santa Barbara, CA 93101
Tel. (805) 963-7289; Fax (805) 963-0230
E-mail: CulinarArt@aol.com

Culinary Tours with Burton Anderson: Treasures of the Italian and Mediterranean Table
Hamilton Fitzjames
1011 Upper Middle Road E., Suite 1158
Oakville, ON, Canada L6H 5Z9
Tel. (905) 842-1845 or (800) 801-6147; Fax (905) 842-2196
E-mail: HamiltonFitzjamesAmerica@compuserve.com

Truffle excursions in Piedmont
Alberto Romagnola, I Viaggi del Tartufo
Via General Govone 5/a
12051 Alba (CN), Italy
Tel. (01139) 0173.29.31.61;
Fax (01139) 0173.36.35.36
E-mail: viaggi.tartufo@isiline.it

**Restaurants**
Al Cavallino Bianco
Via Sbrisi, 2
Polesine Parmense (Emilia-Romagna)
Tel. (01139) 0524.96.136

Da Delfina
Via della Chiesa, 1
Artimino (Tuscany)
Tel. (01139) 055.871.8074;
Fax (01139) 055.871.8175

La Casa di Caccia
Via delle Fornaci, 20
Borgo San Lorenzo (Tuscany)
Tel. (01139) 055.849.5909;
Fax (01139) 055.849.5910

Hosteria Giusti
Via Farini, 75
Modena (Emilia-Romagna)
Tel. (01139) 059.22.25.33

Ristorante Picci
Via XX Settembre
Cavriago (Emilia-Romagna)
Tel. (01139) 0522.37.18.01

Trattoria La Bussola
Via Vecchia Fiorentina, 382
Catena (Tuscany)
Tel. (01139) 0573.74.31.28

**Finding Ingredients in the United States**
Dean & Deluca
560 Broadway
New York, NY 10012
Tel. (212) 226-6800
Catalog Tel. (800) 221-7714
Balsamic vinegars, artisanal pasta, capers, risotto

Di Palo Fine Foods
206 Grand Street
New York, NY 10013
Tel. (212) 226-1033
Parmigiano-Reggiano, other imported and handmade cheeses

Food Matters
Box 99707
Emeryville, CA 94608
Tel. (510) 658-7388; Fax (510) 658-7404
Referral to retail sources for mozzarella, caciocavallo, and Parmigiano-Reggiano cheeses

Manicaretti Imports
5332 College Avenue, No. 200
Oakland, CA 94618
Tel. (800) 799-9830
Leonardi balsamic vinegars, Rustichella d'Abruzzo pasta, Principato di Lucedio risotto, Caravaglio capers, and fine olive oils, including agrumato oils

Polarica, Inc.
107 Quint Street
San Francisco, CA 94124
Tel. (800) 426-3872; Fax (415) 647-6826
Specializes in fresh game such as wild boar, guinea hen, deer, and rabbit; fresh porcini and truffles in season

Todaro Bros.
555 Second Avenue
New York, NY 10016
Tel. (212) 679-7766
Domestic and imported Italian cheeses;
prosciutto; truffles products; semolina
and chestnut flour

Urbani Truffles
29-24 40th Avenue
Long Island City, NY 11101
(800) 281-2330
Fresh truffles in season and truffle
products year-round

Zingerman's Delicatessen
422 Detroit Street
Ann Arbor, MI 48104
Tel. (313) 769-1625; Fax (313) 769-1235
Olive oils, artisanal pasta, capers, risotto

**Finding Ingredients in Italy**
Acetaia e Dispensa di Giovanni Leonardi
Via Mazzacavallo, 62
41010 Magreta (Emilia-Romagna)
Tel. (01139) 059.55.43.75
Balsamic vinegar

Family Mori
53040 Palazzone
San Casciano dei Bagni (Tuscany)
Tel. (01139) 0578.56245
Olive Oil

Azienda Agricola Casearia Barlotti
Via Torre di Mare
84063 Paestum/Capaccio Scalo (Campania)
Tel. (01139) 0828.81.11.46
Mozzarella di bufala

Caseificio Notari
via F.lli Rosselli
Cavriago (Emilia-Romagna)
Tel. (01139) 0522.32.13.44
Parmigiano-Reggiano from Vacche Rosse

Roberto Catinari
Via Provinciale, 378
Agliana (Tuscany)
Tel. (01139) 0574.718.506
Chocolate

Fratelli di Gesù
Via Pimentel, 17
70022 Altamura (Apulia)
Tel. (01139) 080.314.1213
Bread of Altamura

Giorgio Marangoni
Corso Cavour, 159
Macerata (Marches)
Tel. (01139) 0733.26.21.97
Chocolate

Salumeria Giusti
Via Farini, 75
Modena (Emilia-Romagna)
Tel. (01139) 059.22.25.33
*Salumi*, cheeses

# BIBLIOGRAPHY

Anderson, Burton. *Treasures of the Italian Table*. New York: William Morrow, 1994.

Bergonzini, Renato. *L'aceto balsamico: Nella tradizione e nella gastronomia*. Vincenza, Italy: Mundici & Zanetti Editori, 1990.

Bonilauri, Franco. *Parmigiano Reggiano: A Symbol of Culture and Civilization*. Reggio Emilia, Italy: Leonardo Arte, 1993.

Campanello, Felice. *I re soli*. Bologna, Italy: Calderini Edagricole, 1984.

Castellucci, Leonardo. *Il tartufo*. Fiesole, Italy: Nardini Editore, 1995.

Cavazzuti, Vittorio. *Aceto balsamico: Tradizione e use di un antico e pregiato condimento*. Fiesole, Italy: Nardini Editore, 1994.

Field, Carol. *The Italian Baker*. New York: HarperCollins, 1985.

——— . *Celebrating Italy*. New York: William Morrow, 1990.

*Il Buon Paese*. Bra, Italy: Slow Food, 1994.

Jenkins, Nancy Harmon. *Flavors of Puglia*. New York: Broadway Books, 1997.

——— . *Flavors of Tuscany*. New York: Broadway Books, 1998.

Johns, Pamela Sheldon. *Balsamico!* Berkeley, Calif.: Ten Speed Press, 1999.

——— . *Parmigiano!* Berkeley, Calif.: Ten Speed Press, 1997.

Menesini, Renzo. *Le erbe aromatiche in cucina*. Lucca, Italy: Fazzi Editore, 1992.

# TABLE OF EQUIVALENTS

The exact equivalents in the following tables have been rounded for convenience.

## Liquid and Dry Measures

| U.S. | Metric |
|------|--------|
| ¼ teaspoon | 1.25 milliliters |
| ½ teaspoon | 2.5 milliliters |
| 1 teaspoon | 5 milliliters |
| 1 tablespoon (3 teaspoons) | 15 milliliters |
| 1 fluid ounce (2 tablespoons) | 30 milliliters |
| ¼ cup | 60 milliliters |
| ⅓ cup | 80 milliliters |
| 1 cup | 240 milliliters |
| 1 pint (2 cups) | 480 milliliters |
| 1 quart (4 cups, 32 ounces) | 960 milliliters |
| 1 gallon (4 quarts) | 3.84 liters |
| 1 ounce (by weight) | 28 grams |
| 1 pound | 454 grams |
| 2.2 pounds | 1 kilogram |

## Oven Temperatures

| Fahrenheit | Celsius | Gas |
|------------|---------|-----|
| 250 | 120 | ½ |
| 275 | 140 | 1 |
| 300 | 150 | 2 |
| 325 | 160 | 3 |
| 350 | 180 | 4 |
| 375 | 190 | 5 |
| 400 | 200 | 6 |
| 425 | 220 | 7 |
| 450 | 230 | 8 |
| 475 | 240 | 9 |
| 500 | 260 | 10 |

## Length Measures

| U.S. | Metric |
|------|--------|
| ⅛ inch | 3 millimeters |
| ¼ inch | 6 millimeters |
| ½ inch | 12 millimeters |
| 1 inch | 2.5 centimeters |